ADOBE PHOT ELEMENTS 2025 PRACTICAL USER GUIDE

Williams John

Table of Contents

Introduction

Every year at this time, Adobe updates the names of Photoshop. The cost of the inexpensive picture and video editing program is far less than that of a membership to Adobe Creative Cloud. What has been added to the upgrades, and is it time for an upgrade? Adobe has infused the program with AI+ in these latest editions, offering additional automated features that make it simpler to correct, enhance, or transform images and videos into artistic creations by resizing, editing, adding music, or incorporating animation.

New picture editing tools in Adobe Photoshop Elements 2025 include the ability to produce a depth-of-field blur using new AI technology or delete undesired items. AI has also released a plethora of new functions, such as the ability to combine photographs and change colors automatically. A brush that only eliminates undesired items from images is one of the other noteworthy new features. With the Object Removal Guided Edit and the new AI-powered Remove tool, you can make anything vanish in a matter of seconds. By selecting a focus point and allowing the AI-powered Depth Blur filter to automatically generate blur where it's needed, Photoshop Elements now gives you exact control over adding a realistic bokeh effect to a photo for a shallow depth of field effect. The ideal finish may be achieved by adjusting specifics like blur strength, focal distance, and focus range. Learning new abilities is necessary to make the most of the new tools that come with new features. Adobe has introduced a number of Guided modifications that walk users through every step required to make necessary modifications, produce original photographs, or apply entertaining effects. While films may be more imaginative by adding titles, effects, transitions, and other tools, photos can be enhanced by adding contemporary textures and graphics.

Using automated selection tools, the user may change the colors of any item in a picture by selecting the colors they wish to modify. Just select a new color, adjust the hue and other parameters, and then apply the modifications to an object. Four new Quick Actions are now available for applying motion effects. You may add animated sparkles, a flashing heart, or an animated frame to an image, or you can give a feeling of camera motion with just one click. Fun graphics may be used to adorn artworks, social media photographs, and other photos, while textured photo backdrops can be used to give photos a more contemporary appearance. Adding parts from other photographs to create something entirely different or merging the topic of one image onto the backdrop of another is another new feature that allows you to combine numerous images into a single picture.

With the help of AI and automation, you can easily fix photos, add motion, and fine-tune specific features to bring your vision to life. With 59 guided edits, you'll learn how to improve your skills in a variety of areas.

Enhance your photos with vibrant and modern graphics and textures, and add stylish effects. Showcase your favorites in photo collages, slideshows, and quote graphic templates, and easily organize them all. You can also use the web and mobile apps to create and manage your content.

Chapter One

Remove Tool

The new AI-powered remove tool in Photoshop Elements allows you to quickly remove unwanted objects from photos. It uses machine learning to analyze and identify objects in your image, and it will seamlessly blend the surrounding background to preserve its overall quality.

The tool is featured in the Advanced and Quick view under Tools. It's the third icon in the Quick view and the second option in the Enhance tools category under the Advanced.

Follow the steps below to activate this feature:

To use the tool, go to the toolbar and select the "Remove" option.

Make sure that the brush size is right for your task. For instance, if you want to cover the entire area, choose a larger size.

In the options, choose the subtraction and add options.

Drag and drop a larger area or select the specific part of the image you want to fix.

Combine Photos

Combine multiple photos seamlessly.

You can create a stunning and never-before-seen image by blending the subject, the background, and other elements from different sources.

Change Object Color

The automatic selection tools allow you to pick the colors that you want to use, as well as refine to match your style.

This feature can be used by following the steps outlined:

To start the change object color workspace, go to the right panel and select the section of the image that you want to change.

You can use the blending mode to apply varying shades of the chosen color. You can also determine its intensity using the Lightness slider.

The option to refine the application of a particular color over a specific area's leftovers or edges is also available.

Depth Blur

With the ability to precisely control the depth of field, you can add a realistic touch to your photos.

Select your preferred focal point and the AI-powered depth blur filter will automatically add a blur just where you need it. Then, adjust other details like the focal range, blur strength, and distance for the ultimate look.

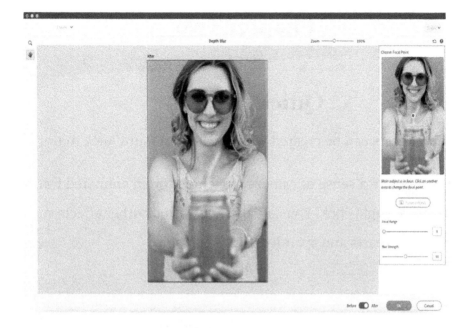

In the Advanced and Quick views, you can explore the options related to depth blur by selecting it from the filters category. You can also perform various actions related to it by choosing it from the AI Edits section.

Chapter Two

Quick Actions

Motion effects can be created with the help of four Quick Actions.

You can create a sense of camera movement or an animated frame with just a single click. You can also add various other effects such as blinking hearts and sparkles using this tool.

Modern Textures and Graphics

You can use the tool's modern graphics and textures to create your own unique visual effects.

Enhance your portfolio with textured backgrounds or create unique social media graphics.

You can add a designer's touch to your photos with vibrant and textured backgrounds. You can also use these to enhance your social media graphics and create unique layouts.

Seamlessly open photos from the Mobile app in a new tab.

Scan the QR code in your photos to transfer them to the Adobe Elements app on your mobile device. You can then access your media library directly from your smartphone camera.

Share via Mobile app (beta)

The Adobe Elements app for mobile lets you easily share your special moments with friends and family using a QR code.

This feature allows you to add a single or multiple media to the Elements app's media library. You can then share these with friends and family using the Share via Mobile app option.

Creative expression is encouraged with the new companion apps for Mobile and Web.

You can try out the new version of the mobile app and upload photos and videos to the Elements media library on the web and desktop. Doing more creative tasks and enhancing your photos on the desktop will also make your experience more enjoyable.

One-click actions can be used to crop, straighten, remove background, and white balance photos.

The basic editing tools for photos include cropping, rotation, transforming, and changing aspect ratios.

Exposure, contrast, highlights, temperature, saturation, and shadows are some of the adjustments that can be made to your photos.

You can create moving and pattern overlays using your photos.

You can also view web-based projects such as photo collages and slideshows through the Elements Mobile app.

You can store up to 2 GB of files on the cloud with free storage.

Web

The new companion app for web lets you access and view the enhanced versions of Elements videos and photos from any browser. It also allows you to create slideshows and collages.

You can add fun patterns to your pictures with the help of the desktop app's advanced features.

You can add a peek-through overlay to your subject to create a depth illusion and frame it.

You can automatically add moving overlays, change the backgrounds, change the text, and share your photos with QR codes.

Make sure that your project is suitable for print or social sharing by applying the appropriate layouts.

You can start your web project using the desktop app and get started with advanced editing.

With 2 GB of free cloud storage, get started quickly.

Chapter Three

Adobe Camera Raw

Since 2004, when it was first compared with Photoshop Elements, Camera Raw has been an indispensable tool for photographers.

We've got you covered. Camera Raw is a powerful tool for creating beautiful and diverse effects in photos.

When it comes to taking photos, you rely on the information captured by your camera to create a unique and beautiful image. A camera raw is a basic form of this process, which shows the light in each spot.

The raw file holds important details about the photo, such as the settings that your camera used when it was taken. Photographers can make numerous changes to this type of file before it is used to create the final product.

The raw file is similar to a photographic negative, which has all the essential information intact.

To find the exact version of Camera Raw that you need, go to the list of supported cameras and lenses.

The term Camera Raw refers to a tool that comes bundled with several Adobe applications. These include Photoshop, Illustrator, and InDesign, and it gives these tools the ability to open and alter photos taken by a digital camera. In addition to raw files, you can also use it to work with regular photos, such as TIFFs and JPEGs.

With Camera Raw, you can use the same tools across different applications, making it an ideal tool for photographers who want to use the same approach to their photos. This is because it allows them to seamlessly work with both regular photos and raw files.

Workspace basics

The easy-to-use interface of Photoshop Elements is designed to help you enhance your photos. There are three different modes that you can use depending on your expertise: Quick, Expert, and guided.

Home screen

The first thing you will see after you open Photoshop Elements is its Home screen, which provides you with a variety of features and tutorials.

The home screen of Photoshop Elements is where you will find the various features and tutorials that are designed to help you improve your skills.

From the Welcome screen, simply tap:

You can use the Photo Editor to create a variety of effects and enhance your photos. To open the photo editor in its default mode, click the icon.

You can click the photo editor's drop-down icon and choose to open either one of the recent opened files or a new one.

Import, organize, or tag your photos.

One of the most useful tools for creating videos is the video editor. It can help you create a variety of movies and creative effects.

To close the welcome screen, go to the upper-right corner and click on the "Close button." It should not be necessary to go back to the Welcome screen to start another workspace. You can open a different one from another workspace.

The settings icon located next to the Close button will allow you to choose which application will start when you open it.

Adobe Photoshop Elements 2018

Photo Editor   ▾   Organizer   Video Editor   ▾

Photoshop Elements window

The eLive view of Photoshop Elements allows you to access the various resources and articles that are available to you through its editor and organizer. It features videos, articles, and tutorials in different channels such as Inspire, News, and Learn. You can also search for specific articles or help pages by typing your query in the search box.

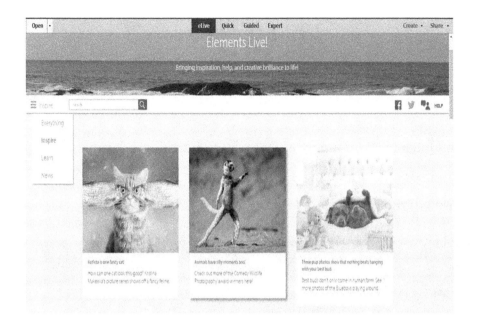

-     Every   article   is   displayed   by   default.
- The following channels are accessible for filtering the articles: Learn, Inspire, and News.

Chapter Four

Quick

The Quick mode is a convenient way to quickly fix various aspects of an image. It can be used to fix the exposure, contrast, and other factors of the image.

Quick mode Guided

This mode allows you to take advantage of the guided approach to editing photos.

In the guided mode, you can easily accomplish predefined effects. Each effect has associated images that will show you the completed task when you hover over it.

Guided mode Expert

You can select the Expert mode to make adjustments to photos.

In the Expert mode, you can create special effects, fix color issues, and enhance photos. In the Quick mode, you can quickly fix common lighting and color issues. The guided mode, on the other hand, provides a variety of tools for basic photo editing.

The Quick or guided modes are ideal if you're new to digital imaging and want to fix issues with photos.

If you're an experienced user of image-editing software, the Expert mode is the right choice. It offers a variety of tools and commands for image correction, including color correction, lighting, and text manipulation.

The Expert workspace can be rearranged to accommodate your needs. You can hide, move, and show panels within the Panel Bin. In addition, you can scroll to different areas of the document and zoom in or out of the picture.

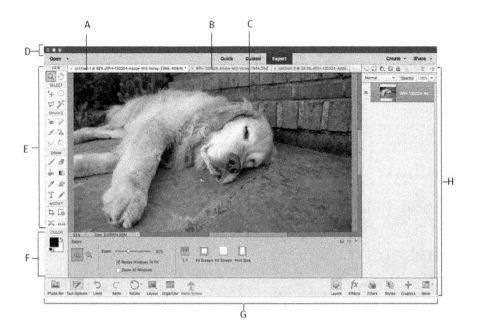

Photoshop Elements in Expert mode

A. Active tab **B.** Inactive tab **C.** Active image area **D.** Options bar **E.** Toolbox **F.** Tool Options bar / Photo bin **G.** Taskbar **H.** Panel bar

Menu bar

The menus are organized based on the task they're assigned to perform. For instance, the Enhance menu has command options that allow you to apply various adjustments to a particular image.

Mode selector

The main interface has buttons that allow you to enter the various editing modes. It also has drop-down menus for recently used files and photo projects.

Toolbox

This holds various tools used in the process of image manipulation.

Panel bin

The various features, actions, and controls are grouped in a logical manner.

Photo Bin / Tools Options

The main interface has a Toggle between the various tools and the photo bin. It allows you to manage the thumbnails of the photos that are currently used and set the options for the selected tool.

Taskbar

The main interface's buttons function as shortcuts for quick access to frequently used actions.

Customize workspace

You can customize the look and feel of the workspace by hiding or showing specific sections.

To hide the photo bin or show the Tool Options, go to the bottom of the screen and select the respective icons.

You can use the Quick mode to split the screen between the original and the edited image. You can also choose the View options in this mode.

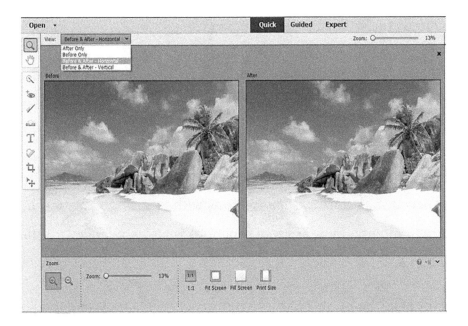

Use context menus

Context menus can be used in the Organizer and Photo Editor workspace. These menus allow you to access the commands related to the active tools or panels.

Position the pointer over a panel or image to use the context menus.

Although some panels do have context menus, not all of them support this feature.

To access the context menus, right-click on the command that you want and choose from the drop-down list.

Use keyboard commands and modifier keys

In the Organizer and Photo Editor shortcuts, you can use keyboard commands to perform various actions without using a menu. The ability to modify the way a tool functions is also available with the modifier keys.

The list of keyboard shortcuts for different types of tools and modes can be found in the section labeled Keys for choosing tools.

Save photos and include in Elements Organizer

You can easily save and include an image in the Elements Organizer if you want it to be included in the workspace.

Go to the Save dialog box and select the option to include an image in the Elements Organizer.

Exit Photoshop Elements

You can exit Photoshop Elements by closing both the Organizer and the Photo Editor. Doing so won't automatically close the former.

Follow these steps from any of the workspace's sections.

In Windows, go to the File > Exit option, and in Mac, choose Quit Photoshop Elements.

To close the workspace, go to the upper-right corner and click the Close button.

When you close Photoshop Elements, choose to save the files that you've modified.

Chapter Five

General preferences

The General category of the Preferences dialog box allows you to customize the way the UI mode works. It also allows you to manage other settings such as the zoom functionality and soft notifications.

How to navigate between the Light and Dark modes

The Preferences dialog box now offers a new option called Light and Dark mode. It lets you alter how the UI mode functions. You may also control other settings with it.

You can change the appearance of the application's UI color mode by going to the Preferences dialog box and selecting the option to switch it to dark or light.

Light mode

Dark mode

Preferences in Photoshop Elements.

Follow these simple steps to switch from dark to light mode in Photoshop Elements.

In the Preferences dialog box, go to the General category and select the option to select the type of Preferences that you want to apply.

You can customize the appearance of the application's UI color mode by going to the Preferences dialog box and selecting the option to switch it to light or dark.

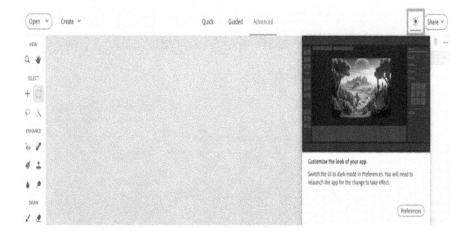

Photoshop Elements offers the option to switch to dark mode.

You can switch to light mode using Photoshop Elements.

Go to the Preferences dialog box and select the desired UI mode from the drop-down list, and thereafter tap OK.

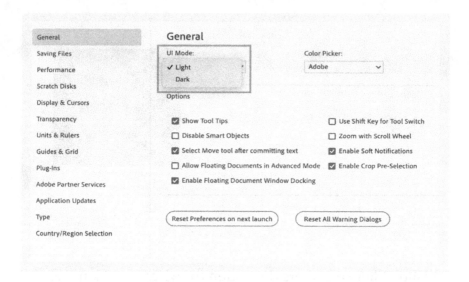

In Adobe Photoshop Elements, you can select the Light or Dark mode.

After selecting OK, a message will appear asking you to relaunch the application.

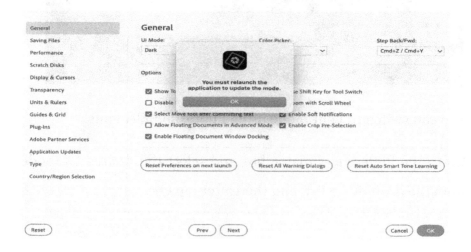

The notification box informs users about the application's relaunch.

The change will be applied once the application has been relaunched.

Saving Files

You can set the preferred method for saving files, such as their default locations and formats.

The "Save As" dialog box can be set to default to the original folder of the file.

Preferences for File Compatibility allow you to set the software's handling of different kinds of files, such as how it opens and saves them.

In Photoshop Elements, you can enable the option to ignore the embedded color profiles in the image file's metadata. This will allow the application to use the default profile for the display and manipulation of the image.

Maximize PSD File Compatibility:

Ensure that the files are compatible with the latest versions of Photoshop and other software from Adobe. This can result in a flattened version of the image and the layers being saved together, resulting in an improved compatibility score.

Never save only the layered files without a copy of the flattened version. Doing so can reduce the size of the file but might cause compatibility issues with older versions of the software.

You'll be prompted to choose whether to maximize the compatibility of your saved files each time.

Performance

| General | Memory Usage | History & Cache |

Saving Files

Performance

Scratch Disks

Display & Cursors

Transparency

Units & Rulers

Guides & Grid

Plug-Ins

Adobe Partner Services

Application Updates

Type

Country/Region Selection

Memory Usage

Available RAM: 14241 MB

Ideal Range: 7833-10254 MB

Let Photoshop Elements Use: 9969   MB (70%)

History & Cache

History States: 50 ∨

Cache Levels: 6 ∨

Graphics Processor Settings

Detected Graphics Processor:

Apple
Apple M1

☑ Use Graphic Processor for improved performance

Description

Use Graphic Processor for improved performance in the following features:
Adjust Facial Features, Depth Blur, Liquify, Moving Elements, Remove Tool

Reset   Prev   Next   Cancel   OK

51

Chapter Six

Performance

The amount of memory allocated for Photoshop Elements will be adjusted.

The cache levels and history states will be adjusted to optimize their performance.

Enable the use of the GPU for enhanced performance when rendering and working with high-quality images, particularly when carrying out complex edits.

Scratch Disks

You can designate which drives should be used as scratch disks to increase the performance of working with massive files.

Display & Cursors

In Photoshop Elements, you can customize the appearance of the interface's display and cursors. You can also specify the way images are displayed.

Painting Cursors:

The default mode shows the tool icon, which is usually a pencil or brush.

The Precise mode shows a crosshair cursor that can be used to precisely place objects.

The Brush Size can be used to visualize the size of the tip. It also helps you see the effect of the stroke.

Other Cursor:

The default cursor icon is shown in the Standard mode.

The Precise mode has a crosshair cursor for different tools apart from painting.

Transparency

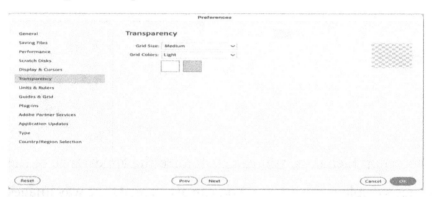

You can set the size of the grid behind transparent areas in your image.

You can enhance the contrast between your workspace and image by choosing the transparency grid's colors.

Units & Rulers

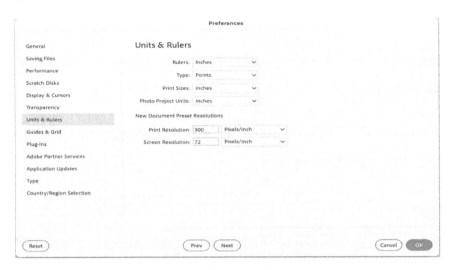

In Photoshop Elements, you can configure the display of rulers and units in your workspace.

Rulers:

Rulers can be displayed in inches, which is ideal for projects that use imperial measurements.

A ruler can be displayed in pixels, ideal when working on web and digital projects that require precise measurements.

Displaying rulers in centimeters is ideal for projects that utilize metric measurements.

Displaying rulers in millimeters for precise measurements is ideal for print design work.

In graphic design and typography, the display of rulers in points is commonly used.

The Picas utility displays rulers in a format commonly used in publishing and print design.

Type:

Rulers can be conveniently displayed in pixels, making them ideal for web and digital projects that need precise pixel measurements.

The points feature is commonly used in graphic design and typography to show rulers.

Rulers can be displayed in millimeters for precise measurements, especially helpful in print design.

Print Size:

Rulers can also be displayed in inches for projects that follow imperial measurements.

A ruler can be displayed in centimeters for projects that take metric measurements.

In millimeters, rulers can be conveniently displayed for precise measurements, particularly helpful in print design.

Photo Project Units:

Rulers can be conveniently displayed in inches for projects that follow the imperial standard.

Rulers can be shown in centimeters, which is useful when working on projects that take measurements using metric methods.

Rulers can be conveniently displayed in millimeters for precise measurements, particularly helpful in print design.

The new document preset resolution option allows you to set the default resolution for that new document.

The Print Resolution setting specifies the resolution that will be used for new print documents, which typically measures in pixels per inch.

High-quality materials such as posters, brochures, and photos can benefit from a resolution of 300 dpi.

The Screen Resolution option specifies the resolution that will be used for documents that are intended for on-screen use. Usually, this resolution is measured in pixels per inch.

This resolution is ideal for most screen and web display applications, as it matches the regular resolution.

Guides & Grid

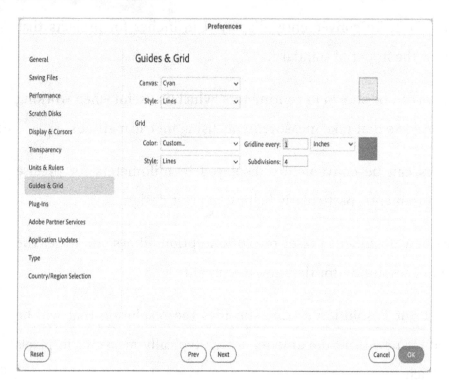

The settings for guides and grids in Photoshop Elements can help you customize their appearance.

Guides:

From the drop-down menu, select a canvas or choose a custom color.

You can choose between a dashed or solid style.

Grid:

You can also choose a custom color from the drop-down list or select a canvas.

Solid or dashed styles are available.

To set the gridline's value, select the units that you want to display, such as inches, centimeters, or pixels.

The number of subdivisions between each gridline can be set.

Plug-Ins

To add more plug-ins, go to the "Select Additional Plug-ins" box and choose "Browse for the desired folder".

Adobe Partner Services

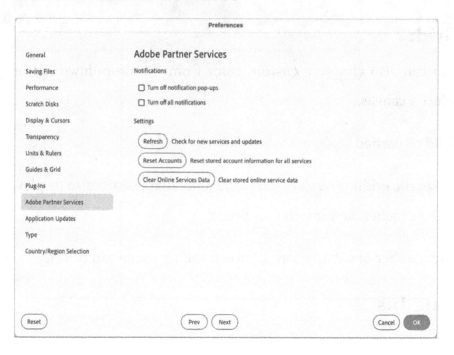

You can disable the notifications sent by Adobe Partners Services when you turn off this option. These may include offers, updates, and other messages from the company.

The option to disable all notifications from the Adobe Partner Services will turn off the various types of alerts and pop-ups.

Application Updates

With the automatic download and installation of updates, you can use Photoshop Elements to get updates without needing to perform any manual intervention.

This setting will notify you whenever a new update is available, and it will let you choose when to download or install it.

You can enable the reminder me later option to allow you to receive notifications regarding updates at a convenient time.

Type

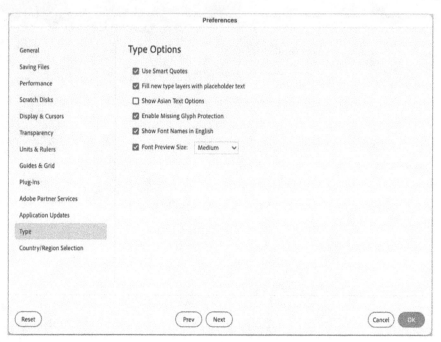

In the Preferences section of Photoshop Elements, you can select the type of approach that will be used to handle text in your projects. This allows you to set the management and rendering parameters that will be used to ensure that your text elements look their best.

When you type, you can automatically replace quotation marks with more accurate typographically correct ones.

In the Preferences section of Photoshop Elements, you can automatically add placeholder text to new type layers. This feature is useful if you want to use sample text in your projects.

You can now show Asian text options in projects that are working with various Asian languages. This allows you to use various types of text, such as vertical.

Enable the protection for missing glyphs. This ensures that placeholders are displayed when the font does not support specific glyphs, which can prevent them from being rendered incorrectly or disappearing completely.

Regardless of the language setting that the font names are set in, this option will let you display their names in English.

The font preview's size can be adjusted in the list to provide a better visual reference when picking a new font. You can select the size that suits your preference when viewing previews.

Country/Region Selection

The geographical location setting can be used to specify which region you want to use Photoshop Elements to work in. This can affect the software's various features, such as content availability and language options.

Chapter Seven

About panels

Although the interface of panels in both Elements Organizer and Photoshop Elements is similar, they behave differently. They are useful tools that help you manage and monitor your images. Some of them have menus that allow you to customize their appearance. You can also organize them in the Expert mode, and they can be saved in the Panel Bin.

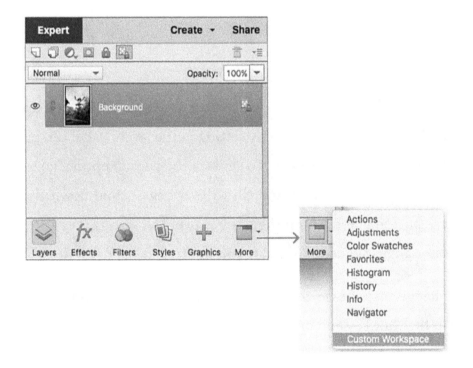

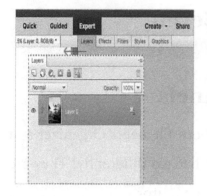 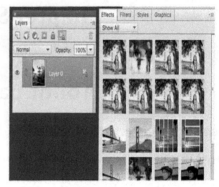

Panel menus

The menu bar and the panel menu have exclusive privileges for certain commands. To view the different options in each panel, click the panel menu.

Pop-up sliders within panels

Some of the settings in the dialog boxes and panels feature pop up sliders. For instance, the Opacity setting in the layers panel can be customized using this feature. To activate the pop-up option, go to the text box's next section and click the triangle. Hold down the mouse button and position the pointer over the setting. Drag the slider or angle radius to the value you want.

To change or increase the values in the pop-up slider box, hold down the shift key and press the up or down arrow keys.

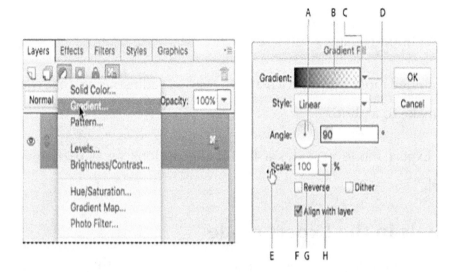

Different ways to enter values

To open a window, click on the "Open" button. You can also go to the text box's next section and click the triangle. You can then choose the value that you want to set by holding down the mouse button and position the pointer over it.

Work with panels

The panels in Photoshop Elements provide various features and information in logical groups for quick access. The Panel Bin is located on the right-hand side of the application. It displays tabs and panels according to the mode that you're in, as well as the kind of elements that you want to work with.

The Quick mode provides a list of effects that can be used to create a quick-mode image.

The guided mode provides a list of the various adjustments that you can make to a photo.

The Expert mode provides a list of the options for a particular panel.

Panels in the Expert mode

The Expert mode allows you to display panels in two different ways: Basic Workspace and Custom Workspace.

Basic Workspace

The default workspace is the Basic Workspace. There are various buttons in this area that are used frequently by the most popular panels. These include Favorites, Effects, and Graphics. To see the other tabs or close them, click the More button.

Custom Workspace

To view the panels using a tabbed layout, go to the Panel Bin and click the arrow next to More. You can then view the various tabs and select one from the list that's available. In the custom workspace, you can keep the panels that are frequently used open. You can also group them together or dock one panel to the bottom of another. Drag and drop the title bar of the tab into the layout or set the tabs dialog box to drop in.

If you want to remove a panel from the Panel Bin, go to the Menu Bar and click the "Remove Panel" button.

The Panel Bin

You can hide or show the Panel Bin by selecting the Window > Panel Bin option.

The Custom Workspace allows you to hide or show the entire panel bin.

Drag the title bar of one of the panels out of the Panel Bin to remove it.

Drag the title bar of one of the panels into the Panel Bin to add it.

To change the appearance of the panels in the Panel Bin, simply drag the title bar of one of them to a different location.

To expand or collapse a panel in the Panel Bin, double click its name.

In the Custom Workspace, you can use the panels that are outside the Panel Bin to work with.

To open a panel, go to the Window menu and choose the name of the one that you want to open. Alternatively, you can click the arrow next to "More" in the taskbar.

You can close a panel by choosing its name from the menu or pressing the Close button in its title bar.

Drag the corners of the panel to change its size.

Drag one panel with multiple tabs onto the target panel's body. A thick line will appear around its center when the pointer is in the right area for the grouping process to occur. You can also move one of the panels to another group by dragging its tab to that part of the group. To separate the panels from one another, drag the one of the tabs outside the group.

Drag the title bar to move a group of panels.

Double-click the title bar or the panel's tab to expand or collapse a group of panels.

Drag the title bar or one of the panels' tabs to the bottom of a stack of panels to place them together. Double lines will appear at the bottom of the targeted panel when the pointer is placed over the correct area.

To change the default positions of panels, go to the Window menu and choose the Reset Panels option.

Chapter Eight

Use the taskbar

The taskbar shows the most frequently used sections and functions while working on images in Photoshop Elements. You can utilize the Tool Options and Photo Bin buttons to switch between the various tools and thumbnails. You can also quickly undo or redo operations related to the layout, rotation, or other features of the panels.

To start the Organizer, go to the main menu, and click the "Tools" button. You can also access the home screen using the "Home Screen" button. In the Expert mode, you can click the arrow next to the More button to learn about the option to switch between the Custom and Basic workspaces.

Use the Photo Bin

The Photo Bin is located above the taskbar and is useful when you want to view photos that have been opened. It can be used to switch between multiple open pictures in your workspace.

The controls of the Photo Bin allow you to hide or open images, rotate or copy an image, and perform other actions. You can also bring multiple open images into Quick Mode for editing. You can create multi-page projects using the Create tab.

The Photo Bin

You can simply perform any of these below:

Windows only users can open an image by dragging it from any location on their computer or other storage device to the Photo Bin.

To show an opened image as the frontmost one, click the thumbnail.

Drag a photo's thumbnails into the Photo Bin to rearrange it. The order in which these are placed does not affect the arrangement of the picture in the Elements Organizer.

Right-click a thumbnail and choose Close in the Photo Bin.

Right-click the photo and choose Minimize under the context menu to hide it in a floating window.

After concealing the image, double-click it and choose Show in the Photo Bin or the Restore option from the context menu.

Right-click the photo's thumbnail and select the "File Info" option from the context menu.

To duplicate an image, go to the context menu and choose "Duplicate". Then, name the file that you want to copy.

Right-click the photo's thumbnail and choose the option to rotate it 90 degrees to the left or right from the context menu.

To view the names of the files in the directory, right-click the photo and select the Show Filenames option from the menu.

To hide or show the photo, go to the Photo Bin taskbar icon and click the "Show" button.

The Photo Bin's flyout menu has additional options that allow you to work with the photos that are currently available in it.

In the Print dialog box, open the Photoshop Elements program and choose the option that you want to print the photos that are currently in the photo Bin.

You can create albums containing the photos in the Photo Bin by right-clicking the photo and choosing "Save As Album." The new album appears in the Organizer.

The Show Grid feature shows a grid-like arrangement of photos in the Photo Bin.

Display the Elements Organizer files in Photo Bin

You can show the open options in the Photoshop Elements program by right-clicking the icon and choosing Show All.

The Show Open dropdown list shows the albums the user has created. Users can select their albums and their contents will be displayed in the Photo Bin. This makes it easier to organize and access the photos within the album.

The Show Selected files option allows users to display specific files in the Elements Organizer.

Go to the Organizer and choose the files that you want to open and modify.

Go back to the editor and select the Show Selected files option in the photo bin.

After you have selected the files, they will be shown in the photo bin.

Chapter Nine

Open files

The Edit workspace in Photoshop Elements provides users with a variety of options when it comes to working with their files. These include exporting, opening, protecting, and processing different types of files. With these tools, users can easily combine different types of files and optimize them in Photoshop Elements.

The Edit workspace can be used to create a blank file or to open a recently used one. It can also customize the type of files that are opened in Photoshop Elements.

The Guided Edit feature is also an additional option that allows users to easily perform various tasks. This tool helps them complete complex editing tasks in a relatively simple manner.

Create a new blank file

If you are planning on creating a web design, a company logo, or a corporate banner, then you might want to start with a blank file.

To create a blank file, go to the File > New > Blank File option.

Select the options that you want to use and click OK.

Name the new image file.

You can set the height, width, and resolution of the images that you want to use for your web design or presentation. You can also choose the size and resolution of the data that you have copied to the clipboard. Base a new image on its resolution and size by selecting its name from the menu's bottom section.

Size

You can choose from the list of standard sizes that are available for the chosen preset.

Width, Height, and Resolution

Unless you have copied the data to the clipboard, the default values will be set based on the last image that you made.

Color Mode

Supports the conversion of an image to either a bitmap, grayscale, or RGB color.

Background Contents

The default color of the image's background layer is white. You can change the background color to use the current one or set it to

Transparent. This will make the layer transparent and replace the background layer with a Layer 1.

Right-click the image's background to choose a custom color or a gray or black background.

Open a file

Import or open files in different formats is available in the Import submenu, the Open As box, and the various dialog boxes.

To open a file in the Elements Organizer, go to the task bar, select the file, and click the Edit option.

Perform any of the following below:

Go to the File > Open option and locate the file that you want to open. If it doesn't appear, go to the Files Of Type menu and choose the All Formats option.

To view recent opened files, go to the Open drop-down, which is located above the tool box.

Drag and drop an image from a directory on your device or computer into the editor.

Proceed to open the file after setting the specific options for each format.

Sometimes, when working with a file, Photoshop Elements might not be able to determine which format to use. For instance, if you're transferring a file from Windows to Mac OS, the format might be incorrectly labeled. You should always specify the correct one.

Open a file in an Application Frame (Mac OS)

In the Application Frame, drag a file from anywhere on your computer to the location where you want to save it. You can also drag pictures from the Internet Explorer's Photo Browser or other storage devices connected to your computer.

Drag and drop multiple images into the Application frame to open them. You can also enable the floating document windows feature to view and arrange them in the Frame.

Open a recently edited file

Navigate to the recently edited file's menu and choose the one you want to open from the drop-down.

In the Open Recently EDITED File submenu, select the number of files you want to open and click the Preferences button. You can also enter the text box in the recent list containing files to get the most recent ones.

Specify the file format in which to open a file

Go to the File > Open As menu and choose the file that you want to open. Then, choose the format that you want to use from the drop-down list.

If the file doesn't open, it might be because the chosen format might not match the actual version of the file.

Open a PDF file

PDF is a widely used file format that can accommodate various types of data, such as images and text. It's the primary choice for the electronic document navigation and search features of Adobe's Acrobat software.

The Import PDF option allows you to preview the entire PDF file and choose whether you want to open it in the Photoshop editor. You can also import just the images from the file.

The import of only the images will not affect the size, resolution, and color mode. On the other hand, if you import entire pages, you can modify the pages' resolution, mode, and size.

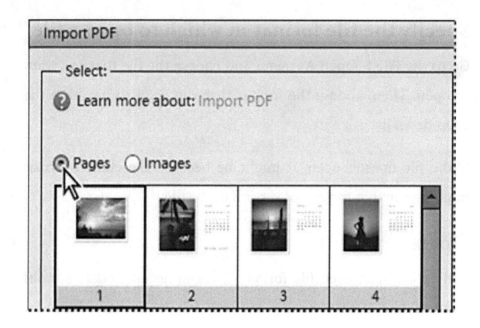

The first thing you see when you open a new page is a list of thumbnails. To increase the size of the page, go to the Thumbnail Size menu and select the option that you want.

After choosing a PDF file, click Open. You may change the type of files that are displayed in the list by pressing the File Of Type option.

Import only the pictures from a PDF file. In the import section, choose the option that you want to use. Then, choose the images that you want to open. You can also select multiple images by holding the Ctrl or Command key. If you want to avoid importing pages, skip this step.

To import specific pages from a PDF file, go to the Import PDF option and choose the option that you want.

If the file has multiple pages, go to the section containing multiple pages and choose which one you want to open. Then, click OK. To open multiple pages, use the command or Ctrl key combination.

To change the name of the file or type a new one in the Name box, go to the Page Options section.

To minimize the jagged edges in the image, use the anti-aliased option. This feature is enabled when the file is bitmapped.

Enable the Constrain Proportions option to prevent the image from getting distorted due to the size of the file.

Change the resolution setting to 300 ppi or type in a new value. A larger resolution will increase the file's size.

You can change the mode of the photos to either maintain the colors or automatically make them white and black. If the file has an embedded profile of the ICC, you can select the option from the menu.

To hide any message that might be displayed during the import process, select the option Suppress Warnings.

After choosing the option, click OK.

Chapter Ten

Place a PDF file in a new layer

Placing a PDF file's pages or images into a new layer can be done with the help of this feature. However, you can't change the text or vector data within the placed artwork because it's bitmapped.

To start the process of placing the artwork, open the image in Photoshop Elements.

Navigate to the File > Place option and choose the file that you want to place.

After selecting the desired page, click OK. If you want to place multiple pages in a PDF file, go to your selected section and choose the one that you want to place.

The artwork that's been placed inside the Photoshop Elements image appears in a bounding box located at the center. It retains its original aspect ratio, but if it's bigger than the image, it can be resized to fit.

Drag and reposition the artwork using the pointer inside the box.

Scale the arrangement of the artwork by doing several steps.

Drag one of the handles from the sides or corners of the box to reposition the artwork.

In the tool options section, enter the values for the height and width of the artwork. These options are usually used to represent the percentage scale. However, you can also enter different units of measurement, such as centimeters, inches, or pixels. To set the artwork's proportions, click the Constrain option.

You can rotate the artwork by doing so in the following way.

Drag the pointer toward the box that's located outside the artwork.

To change the angle of the pointer, go to the options bar, click on the option, and drag it.

Hold down the Ctrl key and drag the box's side handle to distort the artwork.

To blend the edges of the image during the rasterization process, select the option that you want to use. You can then manually set the transition between the two edges during the process.

To add the artwork to a new layer after it's placed, click the Commit option ✔ .

Process multiple files

The command applies to a folder of files. You can also process multiple images if you have a scanner that has a document feeder. You may need to download and install a plug-in module for your digital camera.

When the files are processed, they can be opened, closed, or saved as modified versions. You can also change the originals or leave them unchanged. If you're transferring the processed files to another location, you can create a folder for them in the new folder.

The "Process Multiple Files" command doesn't work on documents with multiple pages.

The command is used to process multiple files. It does not work on documents that have multiple pages.

From the menu item "Process Files," choose the files that you want to process.

Folder

You can browse through the files in your specified folder and select the one that you want to process.

Import

It scans images captured using a scanner or digital camera.

Opened Files

You can specify all subdirectories for the files that you want to process in the specified folder.

Navigate to the destination and select the folder where the files will be stored.

If you're planning on using the folder as the destination, you can also set a file-naming convention for the processed files and choose the appropriate file compatibility options.

In the Rename Files option, select the text or elements from the menus and then enter the fields that you want to be used to combine them into the default names of the files. The fields allow you to change the formatting and order of the files' components. To prevent them from overwriting one another, you should have at least one unique field for each file.

The starting serial number for different fields is specified in the menu item "Starting Serial Number". On the other hand, if you're using the pop-up menu option for the serial letter, the fields will start with "A" for the first file.

Choose "Make files compatible with Windows, Mac, and Unix" to make them compatible with these operating systems.

In the Image Size section, choose the Resize option from the menu. Then, type in the height and width of the photos that you want to be resized. You can also set the Constrain Proportions option to prevent the height and width of the photos from being too different.

You can apply automatic adjustments to the images by selecting the Quick Fix option from the menu.

You can add a label to the photos by choosing the option from the menu's Labels section. You can then customize the various features of the label, such as its text position, size, opacity and font. You can also change the color of the text by pressing the "Color swatch" button.

You can add a permanent watermark to the images with the option "Watermark." This type of effect can be used for various types of photos.

To keep track of all the errors that occurred during the process, select the "Log errors that resulted from processing files" option from the menu. A message will appear after the process has finished if the errors are logged. To review the file, open it with a text editor.

After you've processed the files, click OK to save them.

Close a file

Follow these steps below to get started in Photoshop Elements.

You can decide to choose File > Close. Or choose File > Close All

Make a decision whether to save the file or not. If you want to save the file, click Yes.

To stop the file from being saved, click No.

To apply the current action on all of the files that are currently closed, select the option Apply to All. For instance, if you click Yes to Save the First File, all the other open files will be saved.

The grid and guides settings can be changed.

You can change the guides and grid settings by going to the Edit Preferences section and selecting the Preferences for Guides and Grid.

Navigate to the section labeled "Grids and Guides" and select the Preferences option.

You can pick a preset color or click the swatch to choose a customized one.

The style of the grid can be customized. You can choose between solid and dashed lines. For broken lines, choose the option "Dots".

In the Gridline Every section, enter the value of the number you want to set as the measurement for the spacing of the major grid lines.

In the subdivisions section, enter the value you want to set as the frequency of the minor grid lines.

Modifying the guides and grid settings.

Go to the Edit Preferences section and select the Preferences for the guides and grid.

Navigate to the section labeled "Grids and Guides" and select the Preferences option.

You can choose a preset color or click the swatch to pick a custom one.

You can customize the style of the grid's lines. You can choose between solid and dashed lines. You can also set the spacing of the broken lines.

Enter the value of your choice and the unit of measurement that you want to use to define the major grid lines' spacing.

Enter the value of the number you want to set as the frequency of the minor grid lines in the subdivisions section.

Chapter Eleven

About file information (metadata)

The metadata of an image file is collected when you take a snapshot of your digital camera. It includes details such as the date and time of the photo's capture, the aperture, shutter speed, and the model of the camera. You can view and add this information to your file in the Properties section of the Elements Organizer or the File Info dialog box in Photoshop Elements.

You can add various information to your files, such as the title, descriptions, and keyword tags, to help identify them as you organize and manage your collection. In addition, as you make changes to the file, Photoshop Elements will track its history and add this data to the metadata of the image.

When an image is opened, it will automatically scan for Digimarc copyright watermarks. If detected, the symbol for copyright will be displayed in the title bar of the image. There will also be information about the copyright status, including the URL section, in the File Info box.

You can add a visual watermark to an image to indicate that it is your own work, though this doesn't affect the information in the file. To learn how to create one, refer to the articles below.

Permanent watermarks can be applied to a batch of photos.

Layered text can be used to create a permanent watermark.

You can create a layered text watermark using the Brush tool.

View or add file information

The File Info dialog box shows the information about the camera, including the model, aperture, and caption, as well as the authorship and copyright status of the image. You can add this data to the file using the Extensible Metadata Platform XMP.

The XMP is a standard XML framework that enables the creation and processing of metadata in different formats. It can be used by third-party applications and workflows to standardize the interchange of information in a file. Creating templates for different types of files allows you to add information more quickly.

You are not permitted to modify the metadata of the Camera Data category.

The File Info dialog box in the Photo Browser displays the tags that have been added to a file as keywords. However, some file formats, such as those used for printing, do not support this feature.

After the image has been opened, go to the File > File Info section and choose the category that's related to the camera data.

You can view or modify the specific information in the Description section by clicking the "Description" button at the top-most part of the dialog box. You can add or change the document's title, keywords, author information, and copyright status. You can also click the "Add" button to embed the data.

Use the Info panel

The Expert mode shows information about the file and the color value under the pointer. The panel also provides other details depending on the tool used.

To view or modify the information in the Info panel, make sure that it's visible in the area where you're working.

To view or modify the information in the Info panel, go to the Window > Info (F8) option.

Select a tool.

Drag or move the pointer to the image or within it to use the tool. Depending on the type of tool you're using, the following information might appear.

The values for the various colors under the pointer are shown in the color section.

The coordinates of the pointer and the various colors under it are also shown in the color section.

The height and width of an active selection or a particular shape or feature are shown as you drag it.

The starting position and the y and x coordinates of the object you're working on are shown in the orientation section.

The position of the object or feature you're working on changes as you drag it.

The angle of a gradient or line, as well as its change as you drag a layer, shape, or selection, is shown. The distance shown is the change in position as you rotate the object.

The percentage change in height and width as you scale a layer, a shape, or a selection.

The angle of vertical or horizontal skew when skewing a selection, shape, or layer.

In the Info panel, you can set the parameters of measurement units and color modes.

Perform any of the following listed below:

You can change the mode of the values displayed in the pop-up menu by selecting a preference from the drop-down list. You can also go to the More menu and select a color option for the first and second color readouts.

Grayscale

The grayscale values under the pointer can be displayed.

RGB Color

The values of the various colors under the pointer, such as red, blue, and green, are shown.

Web Color

The hexadecimal code for the values of the RGB color scheme is displayed under the pointer.

SB Color

The HSB values for the various colors, such as saturation, brightness, andhue, are shown under the pointer.

You can change the unit that's displayed for the measurement you want to make. You can do so by selecting the option from the pop-up list or the More menu.

Display file information in the Info panel or status bar

The status bar or the Info panel can be used to display different information about a particular file. The leftmost section shows the current magnification, while the rightmost section displays the current file's information.

Go to the More menu and select the option that you want to display in the Info panel.

Select a view option:

Document Sizes

The information displayed in the Info panel shows the total amount of data that's in the image. The leftmost number indicates the printing size of the file, while the rightmost one shows the actual size, including the layers.

Document Profile

The name of the profile used for the image's color is shown.

Document Dimensions

The current selection of the units displays the size of the image.

Scratch Sizes

The space and RAM used by Photoshop Elements in the processing of the image are shown. Left indicates the current amount of memory that the application is using, while right shows the available RAM.

Efficiency

The percentage of the time that it takes to perform an operation is shown, as opposed to the amount of time that it takes to write to the scratch disk.

Timing

The last operation detail is displayed, showing the time it took to complete the task.

Current Tool

The name of the active tool is also displayed.

Save or delete metadata templates

You can save the entries in your metadata templates if you frequently enter them. These templates can be used to enter information in the File Info box, and they can help you save the effort of retyping them. You can also search for related metadata in the photo browser.

Navigate to the File Info dialog box and choose the category that you want to view.

To save the metadata as a template, go to the File Info dialog box, select Export, and then enter the name of the template that you want to save.

To remove a template, go to the Show Templates Folder and select the one that you want to remove.

Use a saved metadata template

Go to the File Info box and choose the Import option.

After selecting the import option, click OK.

After choosing a template from the saved metadata templates, click the "Open" button.

Chapter Twelve

About presets

Pop up panels are displayed in the Tool Options bar, and they allow you to access predefined libraries of various types of brushes, gradients, patterns, and color swatches. The selected presets are then displayed in a thumbnail image once closed.

You may choose to modify the way that the pop-up panel displays pre-defined preset categories. For instance, you can use the names, icons, and thumbnails to display them.

The Presets Manager can be used to load different libraries. The files that are associated with these libraries are located in the folder named "Presets" in the application folder of Photoshop Elements.

Use preset tool options

The first thing you need to do is choose the type of tool that you want to use.

Go to the Options bar and click on the pop-up panel. You will only see the specific tools with this type of feature.

Do any of the following below:

To see and select the libraries that are currently loaded, go to the menu item that appears.

Select a preset by clicking on it in the library.

Go to the pop-up menu and choose the Save Brush option. Then, enter the name that you want to be associated with it.

To save a pattern or gradient, go to the panel's menu and choose the New Pattern or Gradient option. Then, enter a name in the box provided.

To change the name of a panel's brush, gradient, and pattern, open the menu item and choose the Rename option. Then, click OK.

To remove a particular type of gradient, brush, or pattern from one of the panels, go to the pop up menu, select an item from the list, and then click the Delete command. Alternatively, you can hold down the Alt key and click a gradient or brush.

The pop-up panel's menu has a variety of options that allow you to save a collection of patterns, brushes, or gradients. In the drop-down menu, choose the "Save" option, enter the name of the file, and then click OK.

Load a collection of gradients, patterns, or brushes by choosing the Load command and then selecting the desired library file.

The Load command can add a new brush library to your current collection. If you select a preset library, it will replace the current set of brushes that you have.

To add objects from a collection to an existing library, go to the Append section and select the appropriate file.

To replace the current collection of gradients in one of the panels, open the menu, choose the library that you want to load, and click OK. There are also multiple options that allow you to browse and select a library file.

To change the current selection of patterns or brushes in a panel, go to the menu item Brushes and choose the desired library.

You can replace the current selection of gradients, patterns, or brushes with a new set by going to the pop-up menu and choosing the Preset Manager option. This will load a different set of patterns, gradients, or brushes.

The default set of brushes will be loaded if the pop-up panel menu is opened and the Reset command is selected.

The items displayed in the pop-up menu can be changed.

Effect one of the following:

To change the appearance of one panel, go to your desired panel's menu item and click the menu icon located at the upper-right portion of the pop-up window.

To change the display of each panel, go to the Edit > Preset Manager and click the More button.

Pick a view option:

Text Only

The name of each item is displayed.

Stroke Thumbnail

The pop-up menu shows a selection of sample brush strokes and brush thumbnails. This only works with certain brushes.

Although the above options are displayed for the pop-up panels, they may not work for all of them.

Use the Preset Manager

The Preset Manager is a tool that allows you to manage the libraries of various types of pre-defined objects, such as gradients, colors, effects, and patterns, in Photoshop Elements. You can also create a set of favorite or restore the default packs.

Library types are files with their own default folder and extension. Preset files are also installed on your computer. The program that houses the Presets folder is Photoshop Elements.

To remove a preset, go to the Preset Manager's menu and click the Delete button. You can also click the Reset option to restore the selected items to the original library.

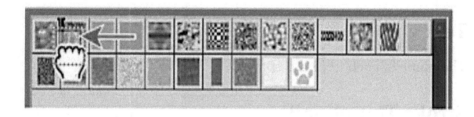

Shifting or dragging a preset using the Preset Manager to a different location

Load a library

Select the Styles, Effects, Swatches, or Gradients you want from the menu item Preset Type.

Do one of the following:

After you've selected a library, click the Load button and choose the destination of your choice from the list. If you're transferring a library to another folder, select it from the list and navigate to that folder. The default is that the files are installed in the Presets folder of Photoshop Elements.

Go to the More button and choose the desired library from the menu's bottom section.

After you've finished, click the Done button.

If the current library has been damaged

Go to the menu item that appears and choose the command that you want to use.

Reset

The default library for this type will be restored.

A subset of the default library may be saved.

In the Preset Manager, select the multiple non-contiguous items or the multiple contiguous ones. The selected ones will be saved in the new library.

Go to the Save Set and enter the name of the library that you want to save. If you want to use a different folder for the library, navigate to that folder first.

Rename a preset

Navigate to the Preset manager and choose the type of library you want to use and the path where you want to save it.

To change the name of the preset, select it in the list and click the Rename button.

To save a preset, double-click it in the list.

New names must be entered for the preset if you have multiple presets.

Scratch disks, plug ins, and application updates

When your computer doesn't have enough RAM to run its operations, Photoshop Elements will use a scratch disk. It's a type of free storage device, and it can be any partition or drive with free space. As its primary scratch disk, the operating system is the one that Photoshop uses.

You can change the primary or designate a different type of scratch disk. When the full primary is used, additional disks are used. You can also set the fastest hard drive as the primary scratch disk. Make sure that it has plenty of room for defragmentation.

Follow these guidelines when creating and assigning scratch disks. Doing so will improve the performance of your device.

You should avoid using the same physical drive for creating scratch disks as Photoshop Elements or large files.

It is forbidden to create a scratch disk on the same hard drive that the virtual memory of the operating system uses.

Rather than using a network drive, you should create scratch disks locally.

You can also create scratch disks using media that's non-removable.

A dedicated hard drive or RAID array is optimal for creating and managing large scratch disk collections.

Regularly defragment hard drives with scratch disks to avoid fragmentation. You can also use an empty drive or a device with plenty of free space to avoid this issue.

Change scratch disks

Creating a scratch disk using Photoshop Elements requires a minimum of space on your hard drive. Regularly defragmenting it will ensure that there's enough room for your scratch disks, especially the one that contains your artwork. You can use a utility like Windows Disk Defragment to perform the process.

In both Windows and Mac, go to the Preferences section and select the Performance option.

From the list of scratch disks, choose the type of disks you want to use.

To change the order in which the scratch disks will be used, select a particular one and use the arrow keys in the list below.

After you've selected the desired option, click OK, and then restart Photoshop Elements.

Chapter Thirteen

About plug-in modules

Developers create plug-ins for Photoshop Elements that add various functionalities. There are a variety of import, export, and special-effects plug-ins included with the program, and they're located inside the plug-ins folder.

The installed plug-ins will automatically appear as part of the program's list. There are a variety of export, import, and special-effects plug-ins included with the program.

The import or export options are additionally displayed in the list.

In the Save As and Open dialog boxes, you can add filters to the menu or the File formats.

If you install several plug-ins, you might not be able to see all of them in the appropriate menus of Photoshop Elements. To prevent this, you should add a tilde character to the start of the plug-in folder or name. The program will ignore files with this character while it's running. To view information about the installed plug-ins, go to the Help section and select the one that you want.

Optional plug-ins are also available. To use them, you must first copy the module from the optional folder into the relevant subfolder. Then, install and relaunch the plug-in.

You can create a shortcut for a specific plug-in that's stored in another application's directory and use it with Photoshop Elements.

Install plug in modules

Do one of the following:

If the installer is included, use it.

Follow the installer's instructions to install the plug-in.

Copy the plug-ins' uncompressed files to the appropriate location in Photoshop Elements' directory.

Pick an additional or extra plug ins folder

The option to create a separate folder for plug-ins that are compatible with another program is also available.

To navigate to the settings for plug-ins, go to the Preferences section of Photoshop Elements and choose "Plug Ins."

In the Preferences section, select the extra plug-ins folder and then click on the "Choose Folder" button.

Double-click the directory where the files are stored to view the contents. The path to the directory will be shown in the Preferences window.

It should be noted that you cannot select a specific location within the plug-ins directory of Photoshop Elements.

After restarting Photoshop Elements, you'll be able to load the plug-ins.

Load default plug-ins only

All plug-ins that are pre-loaded or located in the various plugins-folders of Photoshop Elements are automatically loaded when the program starts. To do so, hold the Shift key while the software is running and press the "Start" button. When prompted, select the option to skip the loading of third-party and optional plug-ins.

Application Updates

The Windows Application Store does not support the option to update the software components of Photoshop Elements.

Update Preferences
○ Automatically download and install updates
◉ Notify me when an update is available

Application update options in the Preferences dialog

In addition to choosing when an update is installed, you can also set the actions related to the update in the Preferences dialog.

To access the program's update options, go to the Preferences window and click on the "Application Updates" tab.

The program automatically downloads and installs updates when it's restarted.

You can notify the user whenever an update is available, allowing them to delay or start the process of getting the latest version.

Undo, redo, or cancel actions

Many of the operations in the Elements Organizer and the Photoshop Elements can be changed or undone. For instance, you can restore the entire image to its old version. Unfortunately, limited memory can prevent you from doing this.

You can either choose to undo or redo an operation by going to the Edit > Undo or Redo options.

To cancel an operation, hold the Esc key until the program stops working.

Using the History panel while editing

The History panel allows you to track the recent state of an image. It displays the changes that have been made to the image in the current work session.

The panel displays the states that apply to the selected or rotated part of an image. You can select which of these states you want to revert the image to.

The History panel does not show the changes that were made to the image due to actions such as scrolling and zooming. These actions do not affect the pixels in the image.

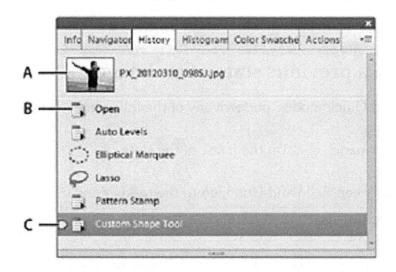

A. Original state **B.** State **C.** Selected state

After closing and reopening the document, the last working session's states are automatically removed from the history panel.

The oldest state appears at the top, while the most recent one falls at the bottom.

The states shown in the history panel are labeled with the name of the command or tool used to modify the image.

A state can be selected to dim the subsequent states of the image. This allows you to see which actions were taken in the selected state and which changes were discarded.

Switching the image eliminates the states that followed it. Likewise, deleting the state completely removes the associated edits.

Revert to a previous state of an image

In Expert and Quick modes, perform any of the following actions.

In the History panel, click on the name of the state.

To switch between Redo and Undo, go to the taskbar and click on the respective buttons.

From the History panel or the Edit menu, choose Redo or Undo.

In the Windows and Mac versions of Photoshop, go to the Edit menu and choose Preferences > General. You can also choose the keyboard command Step Forward and Backward.

From the Undo History panel, choose one or more states to be removed.

Perform any of the following:

Go to the History panel and click on the state that you want to remove. The following states will be deleted as well.

To remove the states from the history panel, go to the panel's menu and choose Clear History. Doing so will free up some memory. It's also useful if you get a message saying that Photoshop Elements is low on resources.

Clearing the History panel is not undoable.

The history and clipboard components use clear memory.

In the Undo History panel, you can remove states and items from the clipboard to free up memory.

In Expert mode, you can perform the following actions.

To remove the contents of the clipboard, go to the Edit menu and choose Clear > Clipboard Contents.

To remove the states from the history panel, go to the panel's menu and choose Clear History. Alternatively, you can select the option from the flyout menu.

To automatically remove the entire memory of both the history and the clipboard, go to your Edit menu and choose "Clear > All."

Viewing images in Expert or Quick modes

The various tools in the toolkit, such as the Zoom tools, the Navigator panel, and the Hand tool, allow you to view different parts of an image using different magnifications.

You can magnify or reduce the view using different methods. The title bar of the window displays the zoom percentage, except when the window is too small.

If you want to view a different part of an image, you can use the window's scroll bars or the Hand tool. You can also drag and pan the image using the Navigator panel.

The Hand tool can be used while another tool is being selected, and you can hold down the space bar to drag the image.

You can drag the Hand tool to examine another part of the image.

Zoom in or out

You can perform these actions by selecting one of the following options.

From the toolbar, choose the Zoom tool and click the "Zoom Out" or "Zoom In" button. You can then click on the area that you want to magnify. Every time you click on the image, it will automatically magnify or reduce it to the next preset percentage. The resulting display will then circle the selected part of the image.

You can also drag the Zoom tool over a part of an image to magnify it. Make sure that the "Zoom In" option is selected in the options bar. To change the position of the zoom icon, start dragging it and hold down the spacebar while moving it to a different location.

You can drag the Zoom slider in the options bar.

In the View options, choose the option to zoom in or out.

In the Zoom options bar, enter the magnification level that you want.

When using Zoom tools, hold down Alt to choose between zooming in and out.

Display an image at 100%

Follow these steps to show an image at 100%.

To double-click the Zoom icon, go to the toolbox and click it.

Select the Zoom or Hand tool and click the "1:1" button in the options bar.

Right-click the image or choose the Actual Pixels option in the View options.

Press Enter to enter the percentage of the image that you want to display.

Fit an image to the screen

Perform any of the following steps below:

Go to the toolbox and double-click the Hand tool.

After you have selected the Zoom or Hand tool, click the "Fit Screen" button in the options bar. Alternatively, right-click the image and select "Fit On Screen."

To determine the fit on screen method, go to the Fit On Screen option in the View menu.

These options will either scale the window size or the zoom level to fit the available screen area.

Resize the window while zooming

When the Zoom tool is active, select the Resize Windows To Fit option in the options bar. It will change the size of the window as you magnify or reduce the image's view.

Windows Resize To Fit will automatically adjust the window size to fit the image regardless of its magnification. This feature can be helpful when you use smaller monitors or work with tiled images.

Chapter Fourteen

Using the Navigator panel

The Navigator panel allows you to change the area of view and magnification of an image. You can do this by typing a value or dragging the Zoom In or Zoom Out button. In the image thumbnail's view box, you can drag it to move the image's perspective. You can also set the view box's boundaries.

You can change the look of the view box by going to the Navigator panel's menu and selecting Panel Options. You can pick a color from the menu or open the Color swatch to pick a custom one.

Open multiple windows of the same image

Navigate to the New Window option in the View menu and choose the image's file name. If the first window is positioned differently from the second, you'll have to move the latter to view the image at the same time.

In Expert mode, you may open several windows to show different views of a specific file. The list of open windows and the thumbnails of each window in the Photo Bin show in the Window menu. With limited memory, you may only open one window at a time.

The New Window option can be used to preview the image's effect in a different window if it's zoomed in.

View and arrange multiple windows

There are two types of options that you can use in Expert mode: View and Arrange Multiple Windows and Open a New Window.

To highlight stacked and cascading windows, go to the Images > Cascade option.

To highlight the edges of your windows, go to the Images > Tile option and choose Edge-to-Edge. As you close the windows, they will be resized to fit the available space.

To compare the magnification of all open images with the active one, go to the Images > Match Zoom option.

To view the same portion of an image in all of the windows, go to the Images > Match Location option. The view will match the active image and the zoom level will not change.

In the Taskbar, go to the Layout option and choose a new method from the pop-up menu.

The Options for Window > Images are only enabled if the preference for enabling Floating Documents in Expert Mode is selected.

Close windows

In Expert mode, you can perform the following actions.

To close the active window, go to the File > Close option.

The Close option will be displayed on the title bar of the window that's active.

To close a thumbnail in the photo bin, right-click it and choose Close.

To close all of the windows open, go to the File > Close All option.

Chapter Fifteen

About image size and resolution

An arrangement of pixels is a measure of the overall width and height of an image. The pixel dimensions are the measurements of the data in the image. For instance, if your digital camera takes a picture with 1500 pixels wide and 1000 high, then the image size and resolution are shown.

The resolution is the overall amount of information that's in a given space, and it's expressed in pixels per inch. High-quality images tend to have better print characteristics.

Even though an image has a certain amount of information, it doesn't have a specific resolution or size. Its physical dimensions can change as its resolution is changed.

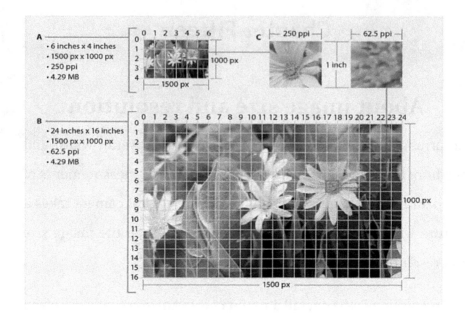

A pair of images with the same file size and resolution but different image sizes and resolutions show that a higher-quality image is better.

The relationship between the resolution and the size of an image can be seen in the dialog box's Image Size section. The value that's changed will affect the other two values.

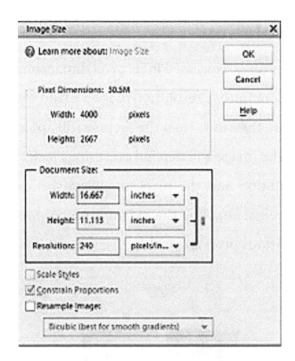

The constraint allows you to change the size of an image without affecting its data.

With the Constrain option enabled, you can maintain the aspect ratio of the image, which is the ratio of its height to width. If you change the resolution or size of the image, it doesn't shrink or stretch.

Resample allows you to change an image's resolution without affecting its data. If you need to use a specific resolution or a larger one than what's allowed, then resampling might degrade the quality of the image.

About monitor resolution

The resolution of your monitor is expressed in its pixel dimensions. For instance, if you set your monitor's resolution to 1600 x 1200, and your photo's dimensions are the same, then the picture will appear on the screen. The size of the image will depend on various factors, such as the monitor resolution and the pixel dimensions of the photo. In Photoshop Elements, enabling the magnification option allows you to work with various pixel sizes.

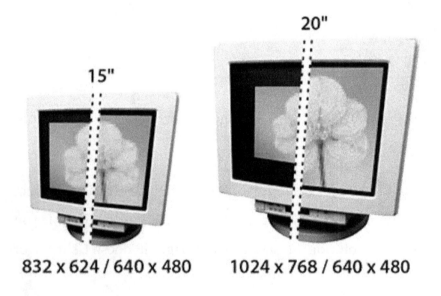

832 x 624 / 640 x 480   1024 x 768 / 640 x 480

An image of 620 x 400 pixels is displayed on different monitors with different resolution and sizes.

You should choose the lowest-resolution option for your intended viewing of the picture.

Display the image size of an open file

Hold down the file information box and view the information about the image. It displays the height and width of the photo, its resolution, and the channel count.

View the print size onscreen

Do one of the following:

You can also choose to view the print size of the image by going to the Print option.

In the options bar, choose the Zoom or Hand tool and click on the Print Size option.

The magnification setting is adjusted to show the actual print size, as indicated in the box labeled Document Size. Be aware that the print size is affected by your monitor's resolution and size.

Modify the print's size and quality without resampling

If you're transferring the image to a shop that requires a specific resolution, then you might need to change the resolution and print dimensions.

This procedure is not necessary if you're printing from Photoshop Elements. You can use the Print dialog box to choose the size of the image and the appropriate resolution.

Resampling is required if you want to change only the resolution or the print dimensions, as well as adjust the overall number of pixels.

Choose Image > Resize > Image Size.

Make sure that the Resample Image option is disabled. You can still change the resolution and the print dimensions without affecting the overall number of pixels, though it might not maintain its current proportions.

You must select the Resample image in order to utilize the Scale Style and Constrain Proportions functions.

Select the Constrain Proportions option to maintain the aspect ratio. This feature updates the width and height automatically as you change the height.

In the Document Size section, enter the new values for the width and height. You can also select a new measurement unit if you want.

Go to the Resolution option and enter the new value. If you want to change the resolution, select another measurement and click OK.

You can try to return the original values in the Image Size dialog box by pressing Alt + Reset.

Resample an image

Resampling is a process that changes the pixel dimensions of a picture. It can affect its overall image quality and print output. When you downscale, this process takes away data from the image.

Upsampling or adding more pixels to an image results in the addition of new ones based on the values of the existing ones, reducing the sharpness and detail in the picture.

To avoid the need to upsample, you can create or scan the image at the appropriate resolution. Resample a duplicate of the file to get a better preview of the effects of changing the pixel dimensions.

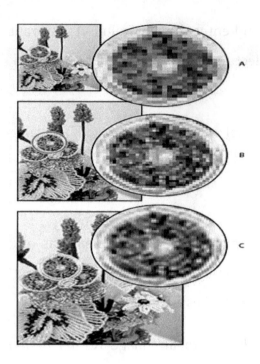

A. Image downsampled **B.** Original image **C.** Image upsampled

When creating web images, you should specify the size of the image in pixels.

To set the size of your image, go to the "Resize" option and choose "Image Size".

Select the "resample image" option and choose an appropriate method for extracting and interpolating.

Nearest Neighbor

This method is generally recommended for working with illustrations that don't have anti-aliased edges. But, it can result in jagged edges, which can appear when performing various manipulations or scaling an image.

Bilinear

Medium-quality

Bicubic

This method is more precise and slower, resulting in a smoother tonal gradation.

Bicubic Smoother

You can use this method when you want to expand images.

Bicubic Sharper

This is useful when you're trying to reduce an image's size. But, it might oversharpen certain parts of the image. You can use Bicubic if this method overdoes it.

To maintain the aspect ratio's current state, select the checkbox that says "Constrain Proportions." This feature updates the height and width automatically as you change it.

In the Pixel Dimensions section, enter the values for Height and Width. You can also select the Percent option to determine the percentage of the current measurements that are related to these values.

The new size of the image is displayed next to the Pixel Dimensions section. The old file size is also shown in the parentheses.

After you've changed the image's pixel dimensions, click OK to resample it.

To get the best results with a smaller image, downsample it and apply the Unsharp Mask. Resample at a higher resolution and produce a bigger one.

Crop an image

The Crop tool will remove the part of the image that's around the selection. It can also focus on your preferred object by removing distracting elements. When you crop a picture, its resolution will remain the same as its original one.

To get rid of a certain annoying background, crop a photograph.

To start with, hit on the Crop tool.

Select the option to crop the image in different proportions from the original one. You can also customize the height and width fields by entering the custom values in the options bar.

No Restriction

This feature lets you change the size of the image to any dimension you want.

Chapter Sixteen

Use Photo Ratio

The aspect ratio of the photo is shown when cropped. The Height and Width fields show the values that were used for the cropped version. The resolution field can be used to change the resolution of the image.

When you specify the values for the height and width of the crop tool, the Custom option is displayed as the selected choice.

Drag over the section of the image that you want to keep. Release the mouse button and the crop marquee will appear as a box with handles at the sides and corners.

You can modify the crop marquee by doing various actions.

To change the aspect ratio, go to the drop-down list in the left-hand panel and select the values that you want to use.

To change the position of the crop marquee, click-drag it to its new location or use the arrow keys to reposition it.

Drag a handle to resize the crop marquee. You can set the proportions using the No Restriction option from the drop-down list. To do so, hold down the Shift key while dragging the corner handle.

To swap the values of the Height and Width fields, go to the options bar and click on the swap icon⇄.

The method for rotating the crop marquee is as follows: Place the pointer outside of the bounding box and drag it↰↓. You can't do this with an image in bitmap mode.

You can change the opacity and color of the crop shield by going to the Preferences menu and selecting the option to customize the settings. You can also set the values for the opacity and color of the shield by going to the Preferences section and selecting the option to customize the settings.

To start the cropping process, click the green button✔ located in the lower right corner of the crop marquee. Double-click the box to finish the process. You can also cancel the operation by pressing the red button🚫 or releasing the Esc option.

Crop to a selection boundary

The Crop tool can remove the areas that are outside the current selection's current boundaries. When you click on the boundary, the image will be trimmed to the selected box. On the other hand, irregular choices, such as the ones made using the Lasso app, will be cropped to a rectangular box. For those who do not want to make a selection, the Photoshop Elements application will trim the image by about 50 pixels from each edge.

Use the Rectangular Marquee or any other selection tool to choose the part of the picture that you want to preserve.

Choose Image > Crop.

Automatic cropping suggestions

The use of the Crop tool is an essential part of any photo editing workflow. With the latest version of Photoshop Elements 13, the application automatically presents four ready-to-Use suggestions, allowing you to choose the best option for your needs. You can also crop as much as you wish, after either taking or rejecting the four suggestions.

Crop an image

The latest version of Photoshop Elements provides four ready-to-use suggestions that will help you choose the ideal option for your needs. After you accept or reject the suggestions, you can then crop the selected part of the image as much as you wish.

Select the image you want to crop from the list in Photoshop Elements. Then, click on the "Preview" button to see the four ready-to-use suggestions. You can then either accept or reject them.

After you have selected the Crop tool, four preview images with the automatic suggestions will be displayed in the Tool Options section.

After you accept or reject the suggestions, you can then choose the ideal option for your needs. You can also look for more suggestions by going to the drop-down list and choosing a different aspect ratio.

You can preview the Crop Suggestions by hovering over them in the options section.

Use grids for better cropping results

Grids can help improve the results of cropping.

Grid Overlay

This feature allows you to set a grid guide for the image and position objects before cropping.

Perspective Crop tool

With the Perspective Crop tool, you can change the perspective of an image by cropping it. This feature is useful if you have an image with distortion, which occurs when an object is taken from a non-straight line or when a large area is photographed using a wide-angle lens.

Navigate to the image in Photoshop Elements and click on "Open."

In the Expert mode, go to the Modify section and select the Perspective Crop option.

You can then draw a boundary or a marquee around the object in question to set the perspective of the image and crop it to the desired area.

You can change the shape of the marquee by using the selection's corners. Hover over any corner and then click and reposition it.

The corners should be moved to align the vertical portion of the marquee with the object or pattern in the photo to make it appear more vertical.

To align the vertical lines, change the shape of the photo's marquee.

In the options section, you can specify the values for the height, width, and height of the image. The resulting image will be adjusted to the specified values.

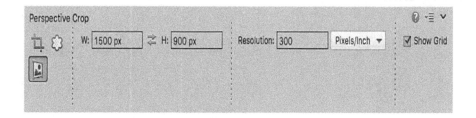

Perspective Crop tool options

You can change the perspective of the image and crop it to the Marquee's region by clicking ✓ on the Transform option.

Use the Cookie Cutter tool

The cookie cutter tool can be used to crop photos into various shapes by dragging them onto your photos. You can also change the size of the box that's used to define the desired area for cropping.

You can use the cookie cutter tool to make a fun shape out of a photo.

Go to the Expert mode and choose the Crop option.

In the Tool Options panel, select the cookie cutter icon and choose a shape. You can also browse through the different libraries in the shapes drop-down.

Select a shape by double-clicking it.

Double-clicking a shape will let you choose it.

Drag the desired shape boundary into the image and then reposition it to the desired location.

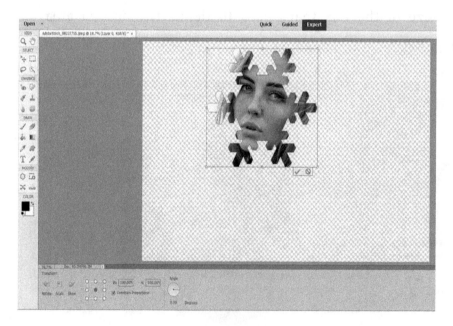

To finish the cropping process, go to the Commit button ✔, or click the Enter key. You can also cancel the operation by pressing the Esc or Cancel option ⊘.

Change the size of the canvas

The canvas is an area within the window that's used to cover an existing image. It can be expanded or decreased in size depending on the side of the image. The added canvas can appear in the background color or the extension color of the selected canvas.

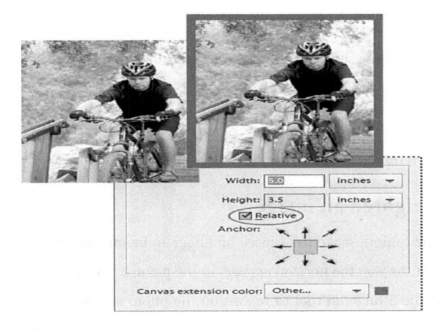

Colored borders can be added to the canvas by increasing its size.

Navigate to the Resize option and choose the canvas size that you want.

Perform any of the following below:

The Height and Width fields are used to enter the dimensions of the canvas. The units of measurement that you want to use are displayed from the drop-down list.

You can also enter the value of the amount that you want to increase or minimize the size of the canvas by selecting the relative corners option. A negative number will be used to decrease the size.

To determine the position that you want on the canvas, click the arrow next to the Anchor icon.

You can change the extension color of the canvas by selecting the option from the menu.

Straighten an image

If the camera shake has caused an image to be misaligned, it can affect the way the horizon appears in the picture. To fix this issue, use the Straighten tool to reposition the photo and get the right angle. You can also crop or resize the canvas to straighten it automatically.

In Quick mode, the Straighten tool is active. When the horizon is visible, draw a line along it. However, if it's not, use the tool to draw a line that's representative of the photo's horizontal axis.

The result is a straight image, and the generated empty edges will automatically be filled depending on the mode that you selected.

You can manually straighten an image using Expert mode.

Select the Straighten option from the menu and follow the steps. You can manually fill the generated empty edges using Expert mode.

The options displayed below will help you choose the right one for your project.

Grow or Shrink Canvas to fit

The canvas can be resized to fit the rotated picture. The corners can then fall out of the current canvas due to the straightening process. The straightened image also has areas of blank background.

Crop To Remove Background

With the option to crop the image, it can remove the background areas that are visible after the straightening process has finished.

Crop To Original Size

The straightened canvas retains the original size while also having areas of white background and some pixels removed.

Creating a cropping and straightening process will help to remove the background.

The three different options for straightening are enabled if the rotation all layers option is enabled.

Navigate to the "Straighten" option and follow the following instructions.

To align the image horizontally, use the horizontal line to draw a parallel line to the right side of the picture. For instance, you can show a train with an incorrectly aligned horizon.

Draw a vertical line perpendicular to the edge of the image to achieve the desired vertical alignment. For instance, if the image shows a crooked tower, you can use the vertical line to show the crooked structure.

Automatically fill empty edges

An enhanced version of the Straighten tool can automatically fill the generated edges with relevant data, instead of using transparent pixels or background color.

Only the original size and grow modes allow the Autofill option. Before you start the process of straightening, select the Autofill option from the menu. When you draw the line, the generated gaps will automatically be filled.

In Quick mode, manually straighten an image.

Navigate to the "Straighten" option and follow the steps.

You can choose from the available buttons to customize the path to the desired effect.

Maintain Canvas Size

The canvas can be re-sized to fit the rotated image. The corners of the canvas are affected by the process of straightening, and the image doesn't have clipped pixels.

Maintain Image Size

The resizing process will remove any areas of the background that become visible after the canvas has been straightened.

Follow these steps to straighten an image. Doing so will maintain the canvas' original size and avoid the appearance of a crooked frame.

To achieve the desired horizontal alignment, draw a horizontal trail along the edge. For instance, the image showing a train with an imbalanced horizon can be depicted with a parallel trail.

To achieve the desired vertical alignment, draw a vertical trail along the edge. For example, if you see a crooked tower, you can show it with a parallel vertical line.

Automatically fill empty edges

When you're ready to start the process of image straightening, select the AutoFill option from the menu. This will automatically fill the generated gaps on the photo's edges.

The latest version of the Straight tool has an enhanced ability that automatically fills the generated edges with related data, without using transparent pixels or backgrounds.

Automatically straighten an image

To remove the canvas from the image and leave it with the flat background, select the "Straighten Image" option from the menu, and then choose "Rotate". The resulting image shows areas of white background, though no pixels are missing.

To automatically crop and straighten the image, go to the image > rotate > straighten and crop option. Notice that the image doesn't have any blank background, although some pixels have been clipped.

Split a scanned picture with several pictures in it.

You can automatically split the multiple photos in a single file into component photos by separating them properly.

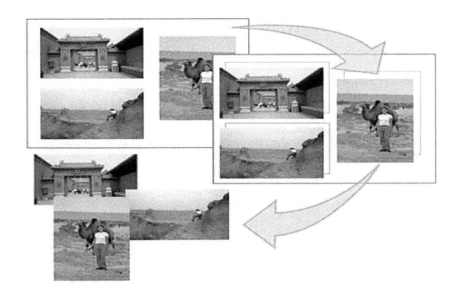

To separate the photos from one page, select the "split" option and then choose "three separate images".

In the image category, choose "divide scanned images". In the process, Photoshop Elements will automatically split the picture into separate files.

This command works best when using a dark paper to cover the white border around the image.

Chapter Seventeen

About camera raw image files

A digital camera takes a picture using its sensor. An image file is usually processed and compressed before it is placed on the device's memory card. But, a camera can also save a raw file without compressing it, which is like a type of negative.

With the help of a camera's raw files, you can easily open and process photos in Photoshop Elements. Doing so allows you to set the appropriate parameters such as white balance, contrast, and saturation.

To use a camera's raw files, set it to save them in its own unique format. Upon downloading the files, they come with various extension names such as NEF, CR2, CRW, and others. Only supported cameras can open these files in Photoshop.

Although you can modify the raw files in Photoshop Elements using the Camera Raw dialog box's features, you won't be able to save your alterations to the original raw file. Instead, you can open the processed version and use the tools to make changes.

Process Versions

Understanding the raw file format with the help of a process version is a good way to work with the latest and greatest features. Photoshop Elements comes with three different versions, and the default one is Process Version 2012.

• Process Version 6

• Process Version 5

• Process Version 4

• Process Version 3 (2012)

• Process Version 2 (2010)

• Process Version 1 (2003)

What Process Version is applied to my image

The default process version of Photoshop Elements when opening raw files that have not been opened in the previous version is 2012. On the other hand, if the files have been opened in an older version of the program, then the older version is used.

To check if the current process version is working on your raw image, go to the Camera Raw 9.1 application's dialog box and click the "Camera Calibration" tab.

If the raw image is not opened with Process Version 2012, the icon located below it indicates that the older version is still being used.

Can I switch between Process Versions?

Go to the Camera Raw 9.1 app's dialog box, click on the "Camera calibration" tab, and then choose the option that you want to use.

Which version is best for you?

Although Process Version 2012 offers the latest features when it comes to processing raw images, you can still use the older version if you have older versions of Photoshop Elements that you've used. Doing so helps maintain the consistency of your old workflow.

The difference between the two process versions is that the newer one has the latest features, while the older one retains the old ones.

The main changes in the 2012 version of Process are the addition of the Whites, Shadows, and Highlights sliders. These new features replace the Fill light, Brightness, and Recovery sliders.

Detail tab:

A new Color Detail slider was added to Process Version 2012. It remains disabled until the feature is modified.

In 2012, two new features were added to the list of sliders: the luminosity contrast and the luminosity detail. These adjustments remain disabled until they are modified.

If you switch to an older version of Photoshop Elements, the newer sliders that are compatible with the latest version will no longer work.

Camera Raw dialog box

The main features of the Basic or Detail tabs are the different controls that you can use to customize the appearance of your image. You can also view the various image settings and tools by clicking on the "More" menu.

You can open and process raw images from a camera. The detail and basic tabs provide the various controls that you can utilize to customize your image's appearance.

Navigate to the Edit workspace and choose the File > Open option.

To open multiple camera raw files, go to the Edit workspace and browse to the files that you want to open.

In the Camera Raw dialog box, you can see the current settings' histogram, which shows the variation in the tone of the image. As you make adjustments, this feature will automatically update.

You can also customize the look of your image using the various controls that are available in the control palette. Some of these include the Zoom tool and the Shadows and Highlights features.

Selecting the preview allows you to preview the image with the changes that you made in the settings. The option to deselect previews the raw image at the current settings and the hidden tabs.

Tap on the Rotate Image keys to turn the image 90 degrees clockwise or 90 degrees counterclockwise ⟲ ⟳.

To apply the settings that were used in the previous raw image, go to the Settings menu and choose the option that you want to use. Doing so will allow you to quickly process your images with the same lighting conditions.

You can set the options to change the white balance in camera raw.

You can also monitor the values of the colors in your image using the tools in the camera raw dialog box. You can position the Zoom, White Balance, and Crop tools to show the colors under the preview image.

You can make various adjustments to your image's tone using the luminosity, exposure, contrast, and saturation sliders.

To make sure that you have all the necessary settings enabled, go to the Auto option and select the "Override" button. Then, select "Restore All Options" and press "Reset."

Do one of the following:

In Photoshop Elements, go to the Open Image option and choose the Camera Raw option. You can then save the modified version as a supported image. The original raw file remains unchanged.

To close the dialog box and cancel the adjustments, go to the "Cancel" button.

To save the changes, click the "Save image" button. You can also choose to save the modified version in a DNG or camera raw file.

The DNG format is proposed by Adobe as the standard for camera raw files. It is useful when preserving the sensor data and other information about the image, such as the type of image and how it should look. You can store the settings in DNG files instead of using sidecar XMP or the camera raw database.

Adjust sharpness in camera raw files

The Sharpness slider can provide you with the desired edge definition by adjusting the image's sharpness. This feature is a variation of the Unsharp Mask filter in Photoshop. It finds differences between the surrounding and outer pixels based on the specified value, and it increases their contrast by the size of the difference.

The settings for sharpening are calculated based on the ISO, exposure compensation, and camera model when opening a camera raw file. You can choose to apply it to all or preview only images.

To get the most out of the sharpening tool, you should first zoom in 100% of the preview image, thereafter, click the Detail tab.

To change the sharpening value, go to the right-hand menu and choose the "Change Sharpness" option. Turning off the option will automatically turn off the sharpening.

If you're not planning on using Photoshop Elements to extensively change the image, you can use the camera raw sharpening slider. Turning off the sharpening will automatically turn off the feature. After all of the other resizing and editing is completed, use the sharpening filters to get the most out of your image.

Reducing noise in camera raw images

The noise reduction controls are located in the detail tab of the Camera Raw dialog. These are the extraneous artifacts that can degrade the quality of an image. The noise includes chroma and grayscale noise, which can make an image look grainy.

To minimize the noise, move the slider for the luminosity smoothing to the right and the one for the chroma noise reduction to the right.

When smoothing or reducing the luminosity or color noise, try to preview the entire image at 100%.

Grayscale noise can be minimized by moving the luminosity smoothing slider to the right.

Save changes to camera raw images

You can use the Camera Raw dialog box to save the changes that you made to a camera raw image. The only difference is that saving the file doesn't automatically open in Photoshop Elements. You can open the raw file using the Open command, which will let you modify and save it like any other image.

You can apply various adjustments to multiple camera raw images by using the Camera Raw dialogue box.

To save the modified version, go to the "Save image" button.

Go to the Save Options dialog box and specify the type of file that you want to save. You can also name the file if you're using more than one camera raw image.

Additional options:

The Fast Load Data option can add a small copy of the raw image to the DNG file to improve the preview speed.

The option known as lossy compression can reduce the size of the DNG file and cause it to lose quality. It's only recommended for raw images that are stored in an archival environment and won't be used for production or printing.

You can also store the original raw data of the camera in the DNG file using the Embed Original Raw option.

When you're done, click save

You can open a raw image from the camera in the Edit workspace.

After you've processed a camera's raw image, go to the Edit workspace and open it.

To apply various adjustments to multiple camera raw images, go to the Camera Raw dialogue box.

After clicking the Open button, the Camera Raw dialog box will close and the photo will be opened in the Edit workspace.

Settings and controls

When you click on the preview image, the next value in the zoom range will be set. You can also use the Zoom tool to zoom in on a specific area by dragging it in the preview image. Double-clicking it will bring it back to 100%.

Hand tool

If the preview image's zoom level is set to 100%, the Hand tool will automatically move the image in the window if it's set to 100%. To fit the preview image, double-click it and hold down the spacebar.

White Balance tool

You can set the area where the neutral gray tone will be set and change the overall color of the image. The values for the temperature and tint will also change according to the adjustment.

Crop tool

The tool can remove a part of the image. Drag it into the preview image and select the part that you want to keep.

Straighten tool

The Straighten tool can straighten or reposition an image depending on its vertical or horizontal orientation. It can also crop or resize the canvas to fit the changes.

Red Eye removal

Red eye removal is applied to flash photos of people and pets with white or green eyes.

The Camera Raw dialog box is opened with the Preferences.

Rotate buttons

The rotation of the image can be done either clockwise or counterclockwise.

Set custom camera settings

When you open a raw file from a camera, the program Photoshop Elements will analyze the information in the file to identify the model of the camera and set the appropriate settings for the image. If you make similar adjustments to the settings of the same camera multiple times, you can modify the default settings of the device.

Simplified Flyout Menu

The Flyout Menu has three-dot options. It can be used to identify the model of the camera, set the appropriate settings, and change the device's default settings.

To use the original settings of Photoshop Elements on your device's camera, tap ☰ and move to the "Reset to Open" option.

To use the default settings of Photoshop Elements for your camera, tap ☰ and navigate to the "Reset to default" option.

To apply the current settings, right-click ☰ the icon and select "Apply Previous Changes."

• Hit the icon ☰ and select Clear Imported Settings to remove the old settings.

Add blur, replace colors, and clone image areas

In addition to these, you can also enhance photos with the help of Photoshop Elements' various tools, such as the Blur, Brush, and Clone. You can use these to add a bit of mystery to your photos or change the colors in them.

Blur or soften edges

The Blur tool can help you soften the edges of an image by reducing the detail. It can also enhance the focus of your subject by blurring the background.

The left and right photos show the effect of blurring the background.

Select the Blur tool 🖌 from the Enhance section under the toolbox or click the R button.

In the options bar, set your preferred options for the Blur tool.

Mode

The option shows the proportion of the pixels that you want to blur and how they will be blended into the rest of the image.

Brush

You can set the type of brush tip that you want to use in the pop-up menu. For more shapes, go to the drop-down and select the brush thumbnail that you want to use.

Size

In the text box, enter the size of the brush that you want to use. Alternatively, you can drag the size slider.

Strength

The value indicated indicates how much blur has been applied with each stroke.

Sample All Layers

Deselect this option and the blur will only cover the active layer.

Drag over the section of the image that you want to blur.

Chapter Eighteen

Replace colors in an image

The ability to replace specific colors in an image is simple with the Color Replacement tool. You can simply paint over a specific color, like yellow, with a different one, like red, in an image. You may also use this tool to correct the colors in the image.

Replacing color

In the Expert Mode, select the Brush tool in the Draw section, or press the B key.

From the options bar, choose the Color Replacement brush.

From the options bar, choose the size of the brush that you want.

For Tolerance, you can specify a low percentage that replaces colors that are similar to the pixels you click. You can also raise the percentage to change the range of colors.

To maintain the blending mode, set it to Color.

To set the limits, select the option from the options bar.

Discontiguous

The option to replace the sampled color in the selected area will be enabled.

The option to replace adjacent colors with the same one under the pointer can be used.

Select one of the sampling methods that you want to use.

Contiguous

Drag the replacement tool to continuously sample the color.

Once

Drag the replacement tool once and only samples the color once.

Background Swatch

Whenever you drag the replacement tool over the background color, it will replace the entire area.

To get a smooth edge over the areas you want to correct, choose the Anti-aliasing option.

To choose the foreground color, go to the options bar and choose the option from the drop-down list.

The Eyedropper tool can be used to select the foreground color.

To change the color, move the mouse pointer over it and press Alt+click.

To change the color, move the mouse over it and press Option+click on Mac.

The Color Picker is a utility that can set the color in your toolbox.

To replace the specified color, drag it within the image.

Clone images or areas in an image

The Clone Stamp tool can be used to duplicate an image or remove imperfections from an image. It can also be used to paint over an image.

The initial picture (top), a person removed using the Clone Stamp tool (bottom), as well as starfish added using the Clone Stamp tool (middle).

In the Expert Mode, choose the Clone Stamp tool from the Enhance section or the Press S key.

In the options bar, set the parameters you want to use for the image.

Brush

To set the tip of the brush, click the arrow next to it. You can then choose one of the categories from the menu and pick a brush thumbnail.

Sample All Layers

To copy and paste data from multiple layers, go to the sample all layers option. On the other hand, to only sample from the active layer, select the option to deselect.

Size

The size of the brush can be set by dragging the slider or entering it in the text box.

Opacity

The opacity of the paint that you apply can be set. The low setting will let the pixels under the stroke show through. You can also enter a value or drag the slider.

Mode

The blending effect determines how the pattern or source will fit with the existing pixels. In normal mode, new pixels will be laid over the old ones.

Aligned

Drag the sample area using the cursor once you start to paint. If you want to remove unwanted parts, such as a rip in a photo, select this option. If Aligned isn't selected, the Clone Stamp will apply the sample from the point where you started to paint. You can also select to copy and paste parts of the same image into different areas.

To set the parameters of the clone overlay, go to the options bar and click on the "Customize" button.

Show Overlay

To show the clone overlay in the size of the brush, select the option to show overlay.

Opacity

Enter the value of the percentage in the Opacity box to set the overlay's opacity.

Clipped

Enable the clip option to clip the overlay onto the brush.

Auto Hide

To hide the overlay while you're painting, select the Auto Hide option.

Invert Overlay

Invert is enabled to change the colors of the overlay.

To start a new sample, go to the section you want to preview and position the pointer on it. Then, click the "Copy" button. You can then copy the pixels from the part of the image you want to paint as you apply the clone.

Perform any of the following:

You can use the tool on the same image and drag or click it.

You can also use the tool on another target image by dragging or clicking it.

Photomerge Style Match

Unfortunately, this tool is not supported by Photoshop Elements 13.

If you prefer an image's style, the tool can be used to add its attributes to another one. You can also work with a group of images and apply styles to get the best results.

The effect won't be cumulative if you apply multiple styles. Only the last one is saved.

After the style has been applied, the image will remain in the same position.

Go to the Enhance > Photomerge > Style Match section and select the image.

To transfer the style, go to the Style bin and add the selected images. Make sure that they have strong details and stylistic traits.

In the Style bin, you can select an image that follows the default style.

Drag and drop the selected image from the Style bin into the placeholder. Alternatively, double-click it in the Style bin and choose the preferred style.

The Edit panel provides you with the necessary tools to refine the image.

Intensity

The intensity or amount of the style that can be transferred is set. The maximum value indicates that you want to transfer all of the style.

Clarity

Enhance the contrast of a stylized image by adding varying intensity regions. This will bring out the details in the dark areas.

Details

This can enhance the global or overall contrast of the image.

Style Eraser

This can remove the specific style that was applied to the image.

Style Painter

Allows you to add the desired style back to the areas where it was previously applied.

Soften Stroke Edges

This softens the hard edges caused by painting and erasing.

Transfer Tones

You can also transfer the style's tones by choosing Transfer Tones. For instance, if the style is white and black, and the image you want to apply photomerge style transfer on is colored, you can select the transfer tone to the colored one.

The original colored image can be transformed into a white and black through the use of transfer tones.

To update the image, click Done.

Adjust color and tonality using the Smart Brush tools

The Smart Brush and the Detail tools can also be used to add various effects to a photo. These tools allow you to select a preset adjustment and then apply the desired correction. You can also use these tools to create adjustment layers, which are automatically created. This feature allows you to reuse the original image layer without erasing any information.

The Smart Brush tool determines an appropriate selection based on the texture and color of the object in your image. It then applies the desired adjustment to the selected part of the picture. Aside from this, you can also apply various other effects such as contrasts, shadows, highlights, and colors.

Smart Brush tool applying an adjustment selection

Select the Smart Brush tool from the drop-down list. Based on the object's texture and color, this tool will determine which adjustment to apply to the part of the picture that you want. You can also apply other effects such as highlights, shadows, and contrasts.

In the drop-down menu, select the effect that you want to apply and then choose the objects in the frame that you want to use it on.

You can utilize the preset patterns and effects with the help of smart brushes.

Available presets

You can't change the settings of the effect because it's a pixel layer instead of an adjustment layer.

Textures option

Presets for texture effects are included to give your images various effects.

Give boring and dull backgrounds a boost.

A satin effect is created for textiles and clothes in an image.

Flowery patterns can be added to dresses in an image.

Designer patterns can be added to a wall or a background in an image.

With the help of the Detail Smart Brush tool, you can easily change the details of a photo by painting over the areas that need more attention. This tool comes with a variety of brushes that you can choose from. You can also click on an effect to apply it, and it has settings for both shape and size.

The tool works similarly to a selection. You can refine the size and shape of the selected area by pressing the "Refine Edge" button. To remove it from the selection, go to the "Remove Area" option.

You can also add or subtract from the areas that are being adjusted using the Brush tools. You can have multiple adjustment presets for a single photo, and these are applied to the individual adjustment layer. Each adjustment can be customized.

When a correction is applied, a pin shows where it was applied, and it provides a reference for that particular adjustment. A new one appears every time a different adjustment is applied, making it easier to modify one specific correction.

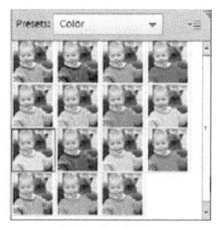

Apply the Smart Brush tools

From the toolbox, choose the Smart Brush or Detail Smart Brush tools.

The pop-up panel shows the presets.

Select the effect that you want from the drop-down list in the options bar.

You can view the different sets of adjustments by choosing an option from the menu. The About presets page provides more information about setting up the pop-up.

You can also change the quality and size of the brush tool by performing the following steps.

In the options bar, open the Brush Picker and choose the settings for the Smart Brush.

If you're a user of the Detail Smart Brush, choose the preset that you want from the pop-up panel. Then, adjust its size in the options bar.

Drag or paint the tool into the picture.

The correction is applied to the adjustment layer, and a color pin appears next to where the brush tool was previously used.

(Optional) You can perform any of the following:

Drag or paint the adjustment you want to add into the picture and select the Add To Selection option if necessary.

To remove certain portions of the current adjustment, go to the Subtract From Selection option and then paint the image.

To apply a particular type of adjustment, go to the New Selection option, select the preset from the pop-up, and then paint the image.

To smooth the selection's edges, go to the options bar and click on the Refine Edges option. Then, choose the settings in the box and click OK. You can also apply feathering and anti-aliasing techniques to smooth the edges.

The last adjustment that you applied using the different tools from the previous session is active if you do so using the Smart Brush or the detail Smart Brush.

Multiple adjustments may be selected if you have several. Doing so will let you modify or add to each adjustment.

Click a pin.

To view the selected adjustment, click the photo and choose the option in the menu's bottom section.

Adjust the correction parameters for the Smart Brush tool.

You perform any of these:

Right-click the pin or an active selection in the image and choose the Change Adjustments option.

Double-click the adjustment layer's thumbnail in the Layers panel.

Double-tap a pin.

After you've adjusted the settings, click OK.

Adjust the correction parameters for the Smart Brush tool.

To open the pop-up list for the preset, click the pin or the active selection.

Select the adjustment preset you want to use from the pop-up list.

Deleting the Smart Brush tool correction

Right-click an active selection or pin and choose Delete Selected Adjustment.

In the layers panel, you can remove Smart Brush's correction by removing the specific layer.

Smart Brush pop-up panel

The Smart Brush and the detail Smart Brush tools in Photoshop Elements allow you to create various adjustments. You can pick the appropriate adjustment from the list in the pop-up menu. The Smart Brush panel can be used to display the selected changes as thumbnails or as a list. In addition, you can drag the picker to its desired location in the workspace.

The Smart Brush panel's specific sets of adjustments can be viewed from the menu located in the upper-left corner. The choices range in tone and form.

About Levels adjustments

The Levels dialog box is an excellent tool for creating color and tone adjustments. It can be used to modify the entire image or a specific section. To access this feature, go to the Enhance > Adjust Lighting tab and select Levels.

The Levels dialog box is useful for creating tone and color adjustments. It can also be used to modify a specific section or entire image.

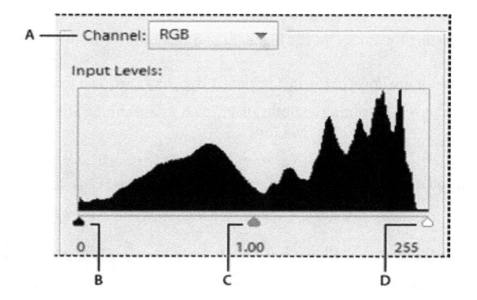

Chapter Nineteen

Levels dialog box

The channels can be used to change the color of the image. The values for the middle tones and shadows can be set.

The highlight and shadow values can be set to ensure that the image uses the full range of tones.

The brightness of the image's middle tones can be adjusted without affecting the values for the highlight and shadow.

Reduce the grays in the image and fix the color cast. You can also enhance it by adding a subtle effect, such as a warming effect, to the sunset.

If you're planning on printing commercial photos, you can enhance the highlights and shadow values with a focus on the RGB values.

Levels allow you to directly work with the image's pixels or through adjustment layers. These provide you with various flexibility options.

Double-click the adjustment layer to open the Levels dialog box and modify the adjustment.

The opacity of adjustment layers can be lowered in the layers panel to reduce their impact on the image.

Multi-adjustment layers can be used to make numerous adjustments without affecting the image.

The adjustment layer's layer mask can be used to confine certain adjustments to a specific part of the image.

Enhance the highlights and shadow details.

Select the Enhance > Adjust Lighting option and then choose the Shadow/Highlights section.

Drag the adjustment sliders or values you want to enter into the text boxes and click OK.

Lighten Shadows

Enhance the shadows and highlight the dark parts of your image by adding a bit of brightness.

Darken Highlights

Darken the light areas in your photos and highlight the highlights that were captured in the image. Pure white areas, on the other hand, don't have any detail.

Midtone Contrast

The value of the middle tones can be reduced or added to the image's contrast. This option is useful if the contrast doesn't look right after you've applied highlights and shadows.

To change the way the image appears in the picture, hold down Alt and then click the Reset button.

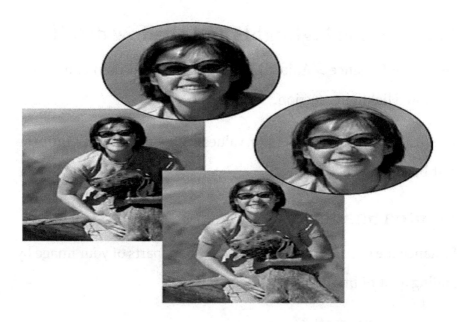

Before and after adjustments can be made to the shadows and highlights. Doing so can reveal more about the part of the face that's behind the sunglasses.

Brightness and shadows can be adjusted using the Levels dialog box.

Perform any of the following:

You can also choose to adjust the lighting levels under the Enhance option.

In the Layers panel, choose the New Adjustment Layer option and then open the existing adjustment layer.

To set the color channel's value to different colors, go to the Channel menu and choose the RGB option. This will affect the three major colors (red, blue, and green) of the image.

Drag the white and black Input Levels sliders to the right and left corners of the histogram's first group of pixels. You can also enter the values directly into the text boxes of the first and third input levels.

To make the picture lighter, drag the highlight slider toward the left.

To see which areas will be highlighted or shadowed, click the Shadow slider and then the Highlight button. Then, press Alt and drag the respective sliders to the left and right. The highlighted and white areas will be highlighted respectively in the individual channels.

To change the midtones' brightness without affecting the highlighted and shadow values, go to the gray Input Levels slider. In the middle section, enter the value of the current midtone.

Histogram displays the adjustment's reflected effect.

To automatically move the Shadow and Highlight sliders to the darkest and brightest points of the channel, click the Auto button. This is similar to using the Auto Levels option, which can potentially change the colors in your image.

Adjust brightness and contrast in selected areas

The Brightness or Contrast command is appropriate for minimizing or adjusting the contrast in an image. It can also be used to change the brightness of a whole image.

Among the following, perform one:

To make adjustments to the image's pixels, go to "Enhance" and choose "Adjust Lighting".

To change the brightness or contrast of a layer, go to the New Adjustment Layer and choose "Brightness/Contrast".

Drag the sliders to change the contrast and brightness. Then, click OK.

Drag to the left to decrease the level, and drag to the right to increase it. The value displayed at the right of each slider shows the contrast or brightness.

Quickly lighten or darken isolated areas

The tools known as the Dodge and the Burn can be used to add details to shadows or highlight specific areas of the image.

The original image is first done using the Burn tool before doing the Dodge tool.

After choosing the appropriate tools, click the "Sponge" button if you don't see the Burn or Dodge tools.

In the options bar, set the parameters for the different tools.

Brushes pop up menu

To set the tip, click the arrow next to the sample. You can then choose from the pop-up menu the category for brushes and choose a thumbnail.

Size

In the text box, enter the size of the brush that you want to use.

Range

The tool will set the image's overall tonal range. You can select the appropriate tone for different areas of the image, such as the middle range of grays and the shadows.

Exposure

The effect of the tool can be set by stroke. Increasing the percentage will add to its effect.

To apply a burn or dodge effect gradually, set the exposure value to a low level and drag several times across the desired area.

Drag the part of your image that you want to change.

Isolated regions should be quickly saturated or desaturated.

If you're not sure which to choose, try searching for the Dodge or Burn tool.

The Sponge tool can be used to desaturate or saturate certain areas of the image. It can also mute or bring out a certain color in an object or region.

The options bar can be used to set the parameters for the different tools.

Brushes pop up menu

To set the tip, go to the sample and click the arrow next to it. You can then choose the category for your preferred brush and then click on the thumbnail.

Size

In the text box or through the slider, you can set the size of the brush.

Mode

This tool will determine whether you want to saturate or desaturate the image.

Flow

The strength of the tool is set by each stroke. Depending on the mode, a higher proportion will increase the saturation. On the other hand, a higher percentage will deaturate the picture.

Adjust facial features

The facial features adjustment process is powered by face-aware technology, allowing you to change or identify the facial characteristics of individuals in a frame. With just a few simple sliders, you can easily alter the facial features of a portrait image.

In the application's settings section, click the "Face Adjustment" button. You'll be able to change or identify the facial features of an individual in a frame.

Make sure that you have at least one face in the picture you want to change. Doing so will ensure that the adjustment works well.

Select the Enhance > Adjust facial features option.

The facial features adjustment dialog shows a circular highlighter highlighting the individual's face, which indicates that the feature recognizes the face in the image.

If there's more than one face in the frame, there will be circular highlighters that indicate that Photoshop Elements has detected faces. To change the features of one or more faces, click a ring or a face.

Pick an individual's face and modify their facial features.

The sliders below allow you to change the various features of a specific face.

Feature	Characteristics
Lips	Smile, Height, Width, Upper lip, Lower lip
Eyes	Height, Width, Size, Tilt, Distance
Nose	Height, Width
Face Shape	Width, Forehead height, Jawbone shape, Chin height
Face Tilt	Angle, Left-Right, Up-Down

In 2021, Photoshop Elements will feature Face Tilt.

The Before/After toggle will let you review the changes that have been made based on the sliders' movement.

The sliders can be used to change the appearance of a specific face.

Double-click the slider to reset the changes to a specific characteristic. These modifications will no longer be applied.

Do one of the following:

To remove the modifications you made to the facial features, select the Reset option.

To apply the modifications you've made, select OK.

Precisely remove red eye

When your subject's eyes are illuminated by the flash of your camera, you might get red eye in most cases. This happens more often when you're taking pictures in a dark room because the iris is wide open. You can minimize this issue by using the camera's red-eye reduction feature.

When importing photos into Elements, you can automatically fix red eye by selecting the "Automatic Fix Red Eyes" option in the Get Pictures dialog box. You may also remove it from the photos in the Browser.

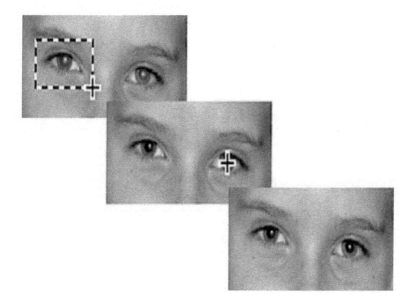

To change the appearance of red eye, go to the top or the center of the image and click on it.

You can manually fix red eye by selecting the Eye tool ⊕ in the Quick or Advanced modes.

In the options bar, choose the Darken Amount and Pupil Radius.

Perform any of the following actions in the image:

A red area in the eye can be selected.

Select the appropriate eye area by drawing a selection.

Release the mouse button and the red disappears from the eyes.

Red eye can be corrected automatically by pressing the Auto Correct option in the options bar.

Remove the Pet Eye effect

The Eye tool can help you remove the red glow from the eyes due to light reflection caused by low light levels or the use of a flash. For animals, the eyes glow green, yellow, red, and white. The commonly used tools for removing red eye may not work properly.

Golden retriever with the pet eye effect (left), and after applying the Pet Eye tool (right)

Choose the Eye Tool from the Quick or Advanced mode in order to correct the Pet Eye effect. Choose the Pet Eye check box from the Tool Options menu.

Do one of the following:

To highlight the eye region, draw a rectangle around it.

Pick the eye in the shot.

Auto Correct will not work after you select the Pet Eye option.

Open closed eyes

You can open a person's closed eyes in photos using the Open Eyes option. You can also use the option to open another individual's eyes in an Elements catalog image.

In the Elements section of Photoshop, go to the photo and open it.

Follow the steps in the Quick or Expert modes to fix the red eye in the image.

To open a person's closed eyes, go to the Options bar, select the Eye tool, and then click the Open Eyes option.

Select Enhance > then Open Closed Eyes.

The Open Eyes dialog shows the person's face with a circular highlighter, which indicates that it's visible in the picture.

In the Try Sample Eyes list, you can select a face that matches the main photo. With the selected face, Photoshop Elements will replace the eyes in the picture.

Do one of the following:

To obtain a source photo from your device, select the computer from the drop-down menu.

To find a source photo, go to the Elements Organizer and select the one you want.

The Photo Bin will let you choose the source photo from the files that are currently open.

You can also select multiple photos from the source to replace the eyes in the main picture. Photoshop Elements will use faces from the photos to fix the closed eyes. You can try different methods to get the best results.

Select the face in the main photo that needs to be opened and click on the various faces from the source. Try varying faces to see which one suits you best.

If the source photo has a skin tone that's different from the main picture, then Photoshop Elements will match the skin tone of the main photo to the eyes.

You may also choose to compare the results before and after the original photo.

If you're not happy with the results, you can try changing the source photo or going for a different approach.

Select OK.

Move and reposition objects

The Content-Aware Move tool can help you move or extend an object in your image.

The original photo shows the kite positioned on the ground. On the other hand, it has been moved to the sky in the image above.

You can use the Content-Aware Move tool ✂ to reposition or extend an object in your image.

You can select a mode that allows you to create a copy of the object or move it.

Move

This feature allows you to change the position of objects within an image.

Extend

This feature allows you to duplicate an object multiple times.

To use this feature, select the type of selection that you want to make.

New

You can drag your mouse around an object to either move or extend it, or create a new selection.

Add

Any selection that you make will add to the previous one.

Subtract

When creating a new selection, the overlapping section of the previous one is taken out of the resulting selection.

Intersect

Creating a new selection while keeping the old one unchanged will only affect the overlapping sections.

Drag the mouse pointer ⚔ over the image and choose the object that you want to extend or move.

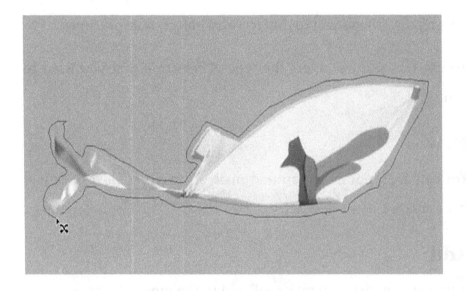

To select the object you want, drag the mouse over it.

After creating a selection, the object should be moved to a new location. Drag it to a new destination.

The selection will be automatically filled in the specified location based on the surrounding image content.

To change the appearance of your selection, go to the new location and choose from the following options.

The ability to rotate your selection in the image allows you to change its angle.

The ability to scale allows you to alter the size of your selected item.

You can change the perspective of the selection in the image with the swipe feature.

If the area that's filled automatically doesn't look right, select the Sample All layers option and then adjust the settings.

Remove spots and unwanted object

The new AI-powered tool that's designed to remove unwanted objects in photos was introduced in Photoshop Elements 2025.

You can use the various tools in Photoshop Elements to remove minor flaws, such as unwanted objects, from your photos.

Remove Tool

The Spot Healing Brush is another tool that can be used to remove minor imperfections from your photos.

Remove Objects with Remove Tool

The new AI-powered tool is designed to automatically remove unwanted objects in photos. It can be used with a single brush stroke to remove the item you want. The surrounding area will be seamlessly blended and filled in order to preserve the details and quality of your image.

The tool is found under the Tools section in the Advanced and Quick views. To use it, go to the left panel and select the "Tools" tab. It's the third icon in Quick view and the second option in Advanced.

From the toolbox, choose the remove tool.

Choose a size of brush that's slightly bigger than the area that you want to fix. This will allow you to cover the entire region with just one click.

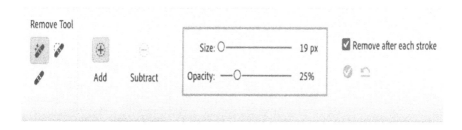

In the tool options, choose the subtraction and add options.

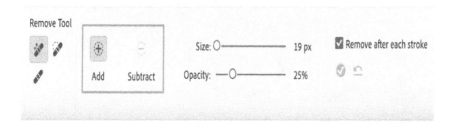

You can apply the change to the entire image by selecting the Sample All layers option.

Drag over or select the desired area to fix in the image.

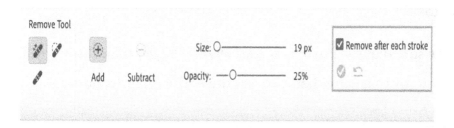

Remove spots and small imperfections

The quick and easy removal of blemishes with the Spot Healing Brush is a good way to get rid of minor imperfections in your photos.

The Spot Healing Brush can be used to easily remove imperfections and blemishes in photos.

You can use the Spot Healing Brush on any imperfection in your photos.

Make sure that the brush is at least slightly bigger than the part you want to fix to ensure that it covers the entire imperfection.

In the options bar, choose the type of brush that you want to use.

Proximity Match

This method will use the pixels around the selection to find a patch that will be used to fix the selected imperfection. If the option doesn't work, try the Create Texture or Edit > Undo.

Create Texture

Using all the pixels in your selection will create a texture that will be used to patch the area. If it doesn't work, attempt dragging it again.

You can apply the change to all of the layers in the image using the Sample All Layers option.

Drag and choose the desired area or change the size of the patch you want to fix.

Use content-aware healing to eliminate undesired items.

You can easily remove unwanted figures or objects from your photos without erasing them. With the Content-Aware option, you can select which objects to remove from a particular image. In addition, Photoshop Elements will compare the nearby content to fill the selected area, keeping key details like the edges and shadows.

Prior to and after the removal of an unwanted object using content-aware fill.

You can easily remove unwanted objects from your photos.

1. Tap on the tool called Spot Healing Brush.
2. From the Tool Options bar, tap Content-Aware.

3. Cover the item you wish to delete from the picture with paint.

Removing small objects from photos is best for Spot Healing. If you're working on a large image, make sure that you have a high-end computer. The requirements for Photoshop Elements will show you if it requires a higher-end model.

Try these strategies if you encounter issues with large images.

In this technique, you can create small brush strokes at a time.

Reduce the image's size.

To relaunch the application, increase the amount of RAM that you have allocated.

Fix large imperfections

When you drag over certain areas of imperfection, the Healing Brush will fix them. You can also remove objects from a regular background.

As you can see, this is before as well as after carefully using Healing Brush.

Select the Healing Brush option from the drop-down list.

From the options bar, select the size of the healing brush that you want to use.

Mode

The mode determines how the pattern or source will blend with the existing pixels. In normal mode, new pixels will be laid over the old ones. In replace mode, you can preserve the texture and grain at the edges of the stroke.

Source

The source for patching pixels is set. The Sampled option will use the current image's pixels, while the Pattern option will use the ones that you specify in the pattern panel.

Aligned

Even if you press the mouse button, the current sampling point will remain the same. You can continue sampling the pixels from the first point even if you stop and resume painting each time.

Sample All Layers

To sample the data from multiple layers, select the Sample All layers option.

To access the sample data, go to any open image and position the pointer.

If you're using a sample from one image and then applying to another, the former should be in the same color mode, except for the one with a Grayscale setting.

Drag over the offending feature and bring it back to life with the sample data. The resulting data will then match the existing elements.

Before you start using the Healing Brush tool, make sure that the area that you want to heal has a strong contrast. Make a bigger selection than the one that you want to heal, and follow the pixels' boundary. The Healing Brush will not bleed colors from the outside if you follow the boundary.

Correct camera distortion

You can fix various camera distortion issues, such as the dark edges caused by lens faults or poor lens shading, by using the correct camera distortion box. For instance, if you take a low-light picture, the corners of the sky appear darker than the center. By changing the midtone and vignette settings, the distortion can be corrected.

The perspective controls can be used to adjust the distortions caused by the vertical or horizontal tilt of the camera. You can also fix the image perspective by rotating it or changing the settings. The correct camera distortion box has a filter image grid that makes the adjustment process easy.

In the correct camera distortion box, select the filter option. It will automatically adjust the distortions caused by the camera's vertical or horizontal tilt.

Go to the preview box and select the option that you want to use.

After you've set the options, select OK.

Remove Distortion

The correct distortion box can fix pincushion or lens barrel distortion. You can type in the number in the box or change the slider's settings to straighten the horizontal and vertical lines.

Vignette Amount

This tool sets the amount of darkening or lightening that will occur along the edge of an image. To set the amount, go to the box and type in the number that you want.

Vignette Midpoint

The width of the area that will be affected by the amount slider is shown. You can set the number to modify the effect on the image's edges or move it.

Vertical Perspective

This tool corrects the perspective of an image by tilt-shifting the camera. You can also set the number to make the vertical lines in the picture parallel.

Horizontal Perspective

Use the slider or the number in the box to change the perspective of the image or create parallel horizontal lines.

Angle

To fix the tilt of the camera or change the perspective after it has been corrected, go to the box, type in the number, or drag the dial to rotate the image.

Scale

The image's pixel dimensions are not changed, though you can change the scale or minimize it. Delete blank areas caused by rotation, perspective corrections, or pincushioning by pressing the box or using the slider. Scaling up can result in cropping and aligning the original dimensions.

Show Grid

When selected, the grid appears and disappears when deactivated.

Zoom

The closer view appears when you zoom in, while the more distant one emerges when you zoom out.

Automatically remove haze

Remove haze, fog, or smog from a photo

This feature can help you remove the dampening effect caused by atmospheric or environmental conditions, specifically when it comes to landscapes. Auto Haze Removal can also reduce the masking effect created by smog, haze, or fog.

The Auto Haze Removal feature is useful when removing haze from photos.

In the Quick or Expert options, open a photo in Photoshop Elements.

After the photo has been opened, go to the Enhance > Auto Haze Removal option.

After processing the image, the effects of fog or haze will be reduced. Repeat this step to continue processing the image.

It is better to use the Auto Haze Removal feature on raw and uncompressed images.

Manually remove haze

An alternative to the automatic haze removal process is to manually remove it.

This particular image was taken during foggy conditions.

Haze removal and extra exposure and contrast adjustments were applied to the photograph.

1. Select the Quick or Advanced mode in Photoshop Elements and open a picture.

2. Choose Haze Removal under Enhance.

3. To get the required degree of haze reduction, apply the Haze Reduction and Sensitivity sliders.

Low amounts of haze removal were used.

Haze Reduction: ⎯⎯⎯○⎯ Sensitivity: ⎯⎯⎯○⎯ Before ◯ After   Cancel   OK

Haze removal is used until the image is more clearer.

Use the appropriate amount of the sensitivity and haze reduction sliders to get the best possible result. Keep in mind that too much of either can cause the image to have a distorted or high contrast.

The Before and After toggles allow you to see how the photo's haze reduction feature performs.

Go to the settings and select "OK." Then, select "Cancel" to stop the edits made using the Auto Haze Removal feature.

Chapter Twenty

Combine Photos

Learn how to easily combine multiple photos into one composition with the help of Combine Photos. This feature will help you seamlessly blend different backgrounds, subjects, and elements from multiple images.

In Photoshop Elements 2025, the Combine Photos feature has been added.

The Combine Photos feature may be used in three places.

In the Guided room of Photoshop Elements, go to the Combine > Combine Photos option.

To navigate to the Combine Photos option, go to the "Image" menu and select "Combine Photos."

In the Organizer section, go to the Edit menu and select the Combine option.

The main steps in the process of combining multiple photos are importing the photos, setting the tone, and then editing each one individually.

Importing a photo

The Import Panel is the first area of the workspace that you can use to pick the photos that you want to combine. It can also help you choose the layout that will be used for the final output.

To begin the process of combining multiple photos, select the ones that you want to use.

You can add photos to the photo bin using the File > Open option or the Open button. You can also drag them to the canvas to use them.

The Import panel can also be used to add photos to the Combine Photos workspace.

You can also add photos from your local drive using the Import panel.

The Elements Organizer app allows you to add photos from the collection.

You can also use the free Adobe Stock photos that are available online.

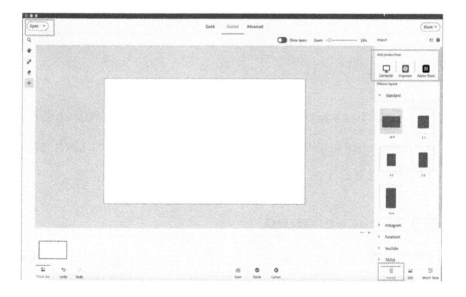

Choose a Layout

The default layout is 16:9, and it can be changed by selecting from among eight different categories, such as Instagram, YouTube, Twitter, and TikTok.

Edit

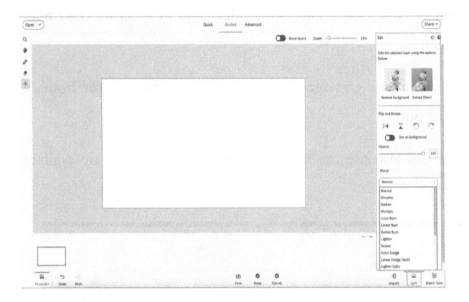

The Edit panel has various options that can be used to customize a photo. These only apply to the selected image. You can click on a photo to select it or use the layers panel toggled on.

Remove Background

This enables you to automatically remove the background from a selected image.

The technique known as reveal allows you to reveal certain parts of the image. On the other hand, the Hide technique hides the rest.

The Size slider can be used to determine the size of the brush strokes on your chosen image.

To get the output from the photo, select Done.

Edit the selected layer using the options below.

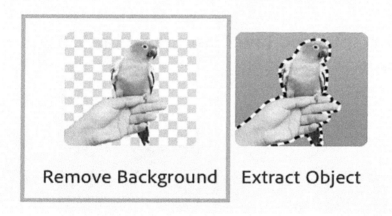

Remove Background | Extract Object

Extract Objects

You can use the Auto Selection feature to create a selection automatically whenever you draw a shape object that you want to pick.

The Quick Selection tool is used to create a selection based on the texture and color similarity of the object that you want to choose. This can be done by either dragging or clicking on it.

You can use the selection brush to add a bit of personality to your chosen object by painting it.

The refine tool can be used to add or remove certain areas from a selection by detecting the edges. This feature is useful for editing and refining your selections.

Edit the selected layer using the options below.

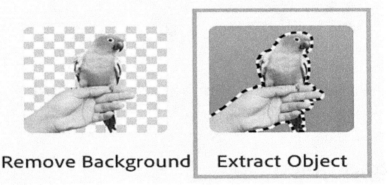

Remove Background   Extract Object

Flip and Rotate

You can choose to flip the image using the vertical or horizontal flip button.

You can also rotate the photo by selecting the right or left rotate button.

Use as Background

You can use this option to add a background to one of the photos. You can also move the image by going to the left panel and selecting the Move tool.

Opacity

The opacity of the selected image can be adjusted using the slider.

Blend

From the drop-down menu, select the option that you want to use to blend the photo.

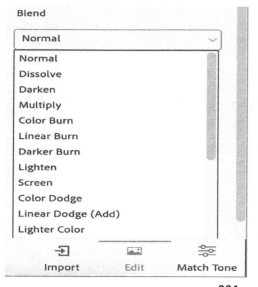

All of the options in the editing section only work on the photo that you've selected. You can click over it to select the one that you want to modify.

Match Tone

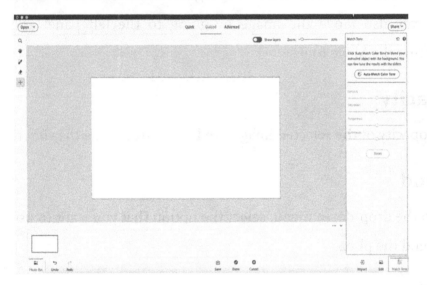

Auto Match Tone

You can use the Auto Match Tone feature to blend the objects in your extracted image with the background.

Use the sliders for temperature, contrast, saturation, and luminosity to fine-tune the results.

To reset your settings, go to the Reset button and click it.

The adjustment sliders will be reset, and the photo will be brought back to the state when Auto Match Tone was used. You can also remove the feature by pressing the Reset Image icon located at the top right corner of the panel.

Additional Tools

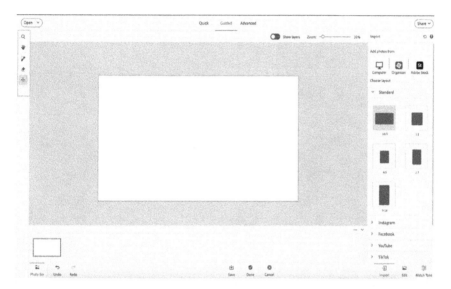

Toolbar on the left:

To pan the selected photo in the canvas, use the hand tool.

The zoom tool allows you to zoom in or out of the selected photo.

The handy spot healing brush can be used to quickly remove blemishes and spots.

The Move tool allows you to move the selected image in the canvas.

www.ingramcontent.com/pod-product-compliance
Lightning Source LLC
Chambersburg PA
CBHW071422050326
40689CB00010B/1940